for ...plishments... your Many ... Dean Graham

America's Poor and the Great Recession

AMERICA'S POOR
AND THE
GREAT RECESSION

Kristin S. Seefeldt and **John D. Graham**

with the assistance of
Gordon Abner
Joe A. Bolinger
Lanlan Xu

Foreword by **Tavis Smiley**

Indiana University Press
Bloomington & Indianapolis

This book is a publication of

Indiana University Press
601 North Morton Street
Bloomington, Indiana 47404–3797 USA

iupress.indiana.edu

Telephone orders   800–842–6796
Fax orders   812–855–7931

Cataloging information is available from the Library of Congress.

ISBN 978-0-253-00967-8 (cloth)
ISBN 978-0-253-00974-6 (paper)
ISBN 978-0-253-00977-7 (e-book)

1 2 3 4 17 16 15 14 13

Contents

Foreword

*I have the audacity to believe that peoples everywhere can
have three meals a day for their bodies, education and culture for
their minds, and dignity, equality, and freedom for their spirits.*

—DR. MARTIN LUTHER KING, JR.

When Dr. Martin Luther King, Jr. accepted the Nobel Peace Prize
in 1964, he spoke of a bold vision in which everyone on earth would
enjoy safety and security. He believed wholeheartedly in a coming
age in which every person would have enough to eat, access to education, and the respect owed to each human being. His statements
echoed those of President Franklin D. Roosevelt, who in 1941 also
called for a future in which people "everywhere in the world" would
experience not only freedom of expression and freedom of religion,
but also freedom from want and freedom from fear.

For both these leaders, the vision of a just and peaceful planet
rested on universal access to basic necessities. FDR and MLK recognized that when people go hungry, when they don't have a decent place
to live, when they can't get access to transportation or medical attention—much less an education or vocation—they are not truly free.

In America today, however, "poverty" has become an impolite
topic. We don't often talk about the poor in mainstream discourse,
and when we do, it is rarely with concern over their standard of living. Far from embracing the idea that everyone deserves to be
treated with dignity, it has become the norm to disparage poor
people as failures, as stupid or lazy, or as criminals or drug users or
frauds exploiting the system. Occasionally, a politician or pundit

makes a nod toward the "deserving poor"—a term that itself demonstrates the contempt in which poor people are held.

More commonly, financial hardship in America is described in terms of a "struggling middle class." The irony of that characterization is that what the middle class is so desperately struggling against—and what portions of it have now fallen into—is poverty.

Facing Facts

What does poverty in America really look like? Together with my abiding friend and public radio co-host, Princeton University Professor Emeritus Cornel West, I set out to answer this question in 2011. Our Poverty Tour took us around the country, meeting and giving voice to our brothers and sisters who are living beneath the poverty line. We sought to hear and share the stories of the men and women, children and seniors, families and individuals who are trying to get by with too little.

Before starting the tour, we needed a clear understanding of the true scope and magnitude of American poverty. We had to know how many people in our towns and cities could not meet their basic needs, and what they had access to in terms of assistance. We wanted a detailed portrait of America's poor—not only the color of their skin, but also how they live and work and take care of their families. We were also determined to understand how the country's present economic conditions and policies were affecting the poor, and what could be done to make those policies more responsive to the needs of low-income Americans.

For this factual foundation, we turned to Indiana University School of Public and Environmental Affairs Dean John D. Graham and Assistant Professor Kristin Seefeldt. Along with their team of graduate assistants, they prepared for us a white paper titled, "At Risk: America's Poor During and After the Great Recession," which formed the basis for this book. Through their rigorous research, they described the characteristics and patterns of American poverty and how these features interact with the country's economic history, reality, and forecast.

What their work revealed was not only informative and illuminating but also atrocious and appalling.

Some 50 million Americans are living in poverty, and that number keeps on growing. Between 2006 and 2010, the number of poor Americans increased by 27% although the country's population only grew by 3.3% during that period. Millions of people who were once solidly middle class can no longer feed their families. More people are experiencing long-term unemployment than at any time since the statistic was first recorded. Fellow citizens hit worst by the Great Recession were those who had historically suffered from previous economic downturns: African Americans, Hispanics, and households headed by women. Poverty grew even faster among children, with 16 million of our precious children—one out of every five—now growing up without enough money for basic necessities like food, clothing, and utilities.

Here in this prosperous nation, we are seeing the type of poverty that is typically associated only with the poorest of developing countries. Close to 3 million American children and their families now live on less than $2 a day.

Poverty, much of it abject poverty, is the new American norm.

Don't Call It a Recovery

There is a strange term that elected officials and media commentators use to describe America's economy after the Great Recession: "jobless recovery." Presumably, someone is making money, but it's not the tens of millions of Americans who want full-time work and can't get it. Talking about a "jobless recovery" misses the point in the same way that talking about a "minimum wage" obscures the need for a "living wage," and referring to the "working poor" ignores the question of why someone who is working is still poor.

What Dean Graham and Professor Seefeldt have done in their analysis is to unflinchingly examine how this "jobless recovery" affects the swelling ranks of the poor. As the researchers so compellingly demonstrate, for those who are already struggling to make ends meet, the hard times are about to get worse.

On The Poverty Tour, we saw firsthand how poor people were living, and we knew that no tiny uptick in the GDP was going to solve their problems. In *America's Poor and the Great Recession*, we learn why this is so: though the poor suffered disproportionately during the recession, they would have suffered more without the

2009 federal stimulus package. These funds have now been expended. State and federal legislatures are scrambling to address their budgets, making cuts to assistance all but inevitable.

Meanwhile, without new jobs, long-term unemployment compounds as job prospects become more remote the longer an individual remains jobless. Additionally, because a number of financial assistance programs are reserved for those with earned income, people who have lost their jobs are also cut off from previously available government resources.

Poor workers employed at the minimum wage may have barely escaped the "jobless" aspect of the economy, but they instead suffer from the "recovery." With their income fixed at $7.25 (or a state-mandated minimum), their earnings are worth less as the economy improves and the value of their paycheck decreases due to inflation.

Shared Security

My goal, along with Professor West, has been to push the topic of poverty to the forefront of American consciousness. Until now, it has been possible for the few who still have means to collectively deny, disregard, and disparage their 50 million fellow citizens who are struggling to break out of poverty. As more and more people who thought they were safe fall backward into insolvency, however, poverty becomes a middle class problem.

We are well past the days of protecting the fragile psyches and delicate sensibilities of those who would turn a blind eye to the poor. When huge swaths of Americans are either entrenched in poverty, or just one layoff or unforeseen expense away from financial crisis, we have no choice but to act. This downward economic spiral is claiming an ever-increasing proportion of Americans, proving at last that what is in the interests of the poor is in everyone's interest. It may have taken the Great Recession for America to finally wake up to the notion that Dr. King and President Roosevelt articulated decades ago, but the country must see it now: There is no security except shared security.

To move forward, we need strategies that are rooted in fact, robust in their impact, and ready for implementation. This is precisely the roadmap offered in *America's Poor and the Great Recession*.

Dean Graham, Professor Seefeldt, and I share a commitment to bringing the crisis of poverty into the light and compelling our elected representatives to correct our broken systems. I have a deep respect and gratitude for the way in which these accomplished researchers have meticulously approached the problem from multiple ideological standpoints. By taking many views into account, they have drafted a plan that is deserving of earnest debate in Congress. I am hopeful and expectant that policymakers will take notice of this important book, and use it as their guide to beginning the process that will, at last, ensure freedom from want in America.

TAVIS SMILEY

Preface

The idea for this book originated in a conversation we had in 2010 with Mr. Tavis Smiley, a distinguished alumnus of the School of Public and Environmental Affairs (SPEA) at Indiana University and a well-known advocate for the interests of low-income Americans. Although Mr. Smiley was concerned about how the "Great Recession" was affecting all Americans, he noticed that the mass media—as well as most elected officials—were talking primarily about the middle class. Mr. Smiley asked us, and a group of graduate students at SPEA, to explore how the Great Recession was affecting the chronically poor, the working poor, the new poor, and the near poor in America.

Mr. Smiley's request led to the publication of *At Risk: America's Poor During and After the Great Recession* (January 2012), a White Paper intended to serve as a factual foundation for his Poverty Tour across the United States (www.thepovertytour.smileyandwest.com). The White Paper was also distributed at a national poverty summit led by Mr. Smiley at George Washington University in early 2011. We are grateful to the following internal and external peer reviewers who provided helpful comments and suggestions on the White Paper that also served to shape the book manuscript: Eric Apaydin, Pardee RAND Graduate School; Sheldon Danziger, University of Michigan; Alison Jacknowitz; American University; Leonard Lopoo, Syracuse University; Austin Nichols, The Urban Institute; Maureen Pirog, Indiana University; Kosali Simon, Indiana University; and James Sullivan, University of Notre Dame. We owe a special thanks to the SPEA doctoral students who helped us prepare the White Paper: Gordon Abner, Joe A. Bolinger, and Lanlan Xu. Their thorough research on poverty data, on the Earned Income Tax Credit, and on housing and the Temporary Assistance for Needy Families program, respectively, were invaluable, and much of what they wrote for the White Paper has been incorporated into this book.

Building on the interest generated by the White Paper, we decided to expand it into a short book, with encouragement from Rebecca Tolen of Indiana University Press. By taking this step, we have strived to create a highly readable book that would be a useful supplementary text in undergraduate and graduate courses on poverty, income security, social welfare, social policy, policy analysis, and public policy. We began by creating Chapter 1, a careful look at the dynamics and employment consequences of the Great Recession, including a comparison with previous recessions. Chapter 2, on poverty, builds on material in the White Paper but includes more depth on long-term trends in poverty, how underemployment is linked to poverty, the structural and behavioral causes of poverty, and forecasts of how the poverty rate may change in the future. Chapter 3, on philanthropy and the poor, is entirely new, drawing heavily on the work of our colleagues at the Indiana University Center on Philanthropy and the experience of Queen Elizabeth I in the sixteenth century. Chapter 4 covers the governmental safety net, with new material on Supplemental Security Income and expanded treatments of the other major federal programs (especially the Supplemental Nutrition Assistance Program, Medicaid, and TANF), and a new section on multiple program participation. Chapter 5 crystallizes our central argument that low-income Americans may prove to be more vulnerable during the slow recovery from the Great Recession than they were at the trough of the downturn. In Chapter 6, we go beyond the White Paper and offer some near-term and long-term reform options for consideration by students, scholars, advocates and policy makers. The reforms we suggest are intended to strengthen the governmental safety net, thereby reducing the hardships that low-income people face during economic downturns and slow recoveries.

We are particularly grateful to Mr. Smiley for his sustained interest in the success of this project and for penning the eloquent Foreword to the book. Mr. Smiley's "co-conspirator" in the Poverty Tour, Professor Cornell West, has also encouraged us along the way and we are grateful for that encouragement. We also owe thanks to Cynthia Mahigian Moorhead of the School of Public and Environmental Affairs, who oversaw the production of the White Paper and worked with us on the production of the manuscript. Special thanks also goes to Luke Shaefer of the University of Michigan who, at the last moment, produced some important analyses for us.

As the book goes to press, there is much uncertainty about where the U.S. and global economies are headed, how the governmental fiscal crises will be addressed, whether the budgetary safeguards for the governmental safety net will be maintained, and what will happen to the well-being of low-income Americans. We trust that our book will shed some light on why the well-being of low-income families is at considerable risk, despite the fact that an economic recovery has been underway since June 2009.

America's Poor and the Great Recession

Introduction

The "Great Recession" officially began in December 2007 and ended in June 2009. A slow recovery is underway, but the severity and extended duration of the downturn have inflicted long-lasting damage on individuals, families, and communities.

This book examines the impact of the Great Recession, including its aftermath, on low-income people in America. Our focus is not only the well-being of the chronically poor but the near poor, the working poor, and the "new poor"—the millions of families who have entered poverty because of the Great Recession's record high levels of long-term unemployment. We explore whether the hardships triggered by the Great Recession have disproportionately affected the same subgroups that have been harmed by previous downturns: men, blacks, Hispanics, young people, and those with few skills and low levels of educational attainment. We also explore regional variations in adversity, highlighting which states and regions of the country have been harmed the worst and the least.

Our focus on the welfare of low-income populations is not intended to deny or overlook the adverse impacts of the Great Recession on other groups in society. Wealthy Americans have watched the value of their stock holdings decline sharply; middle-class Americans may have seen the value of their principal asset, their home, plummet; and working-class Americans, if they have escaped poverty, may have lost their job and been foreclosed upon. Since one book cannot cover everyone, we have chosen to apply what Harvard philosopher John Rawls calls the "difference principle": a special focus on the well-being of the least advantaged group in society, people living in households with low incomes.

The book goes beyond a description of the Great Recession and assesses the performance of America's "safety net": the combination of philanthropic and governmental programs that are designed to protect the well-being of low-income Americans during economic downturns. We seek to determine which programs have worked well and which have worked poorly as the financial hardships of the Great Recession took their toll. We look beyond the 18-month period of the Great Recession and consider its aftermath, including the sobering forecasts of a sluggish recovery for the remainder of the decade.

For impatient readers who like to see the bottom line up front, here are our key conclusions:

1. The Great Recession has left behind the largest number of long-term unemployed people since records were first kept in 1948.

2. One of the reasons the recovery is slow is that recessions rooted in financial crises tend to be deeper and longer, and with slower recoveries, than recessions that originate in other sectors of the economy.

3. Despite the fact that large numbers of Americans were already poor prior to the Great Recession, the number of people living in poverty (almost 50 million as this book went to press) increased during the Great Recession and is expected to continue to increase despite the economic recovery that began in June 2009.

4. The Great Recession has had disproportionate impact on the same subgroups that were harmed in previous post–World War II recessions: men, blacks, Hispanics, young adults, people with few skills and limited education. Indirectly, children have also suffered disproportionate harm. Some states have experienced larger increases in the rate of poverty than others.

5. Charitable donations for human service programs that service the poor declined abruptly in the midst of the Great Recession, as the incomes and wealth of the middle and upper classes declined. Those charitable donations have not yet recovered.

6. Since the onset of the Great Recession, the performance of the U.S. "safety net" has been uneven: federal food programs,

Medicaid, Supplemental Security Income (SSI), and Unemployment Insurance have, for the most part, worked effectively, while federal cash assistance for the nondisabled poor and federal housing programs did not respond much to the burgeoning numbers of families in need of help.

7. The adverse effects of the Great Recession on low-income households would have been much worse had the federal government not responded with large amounts of temporary assistance, largely through the 2009 Recovery Act.

8. Looking forward, fiscal pressures at the federal, state, and local levels of government are likely to lead to cutbacks in the safety net, thereby placing low-income households at greater risk of harm.

9. In the near-term, policy makers can take constructive, incremental steps to further assist low-income families by indexing the federal minimum wage to the rate of inflation, enacting Medicaid reforms that both reduce spending and improve health outcomes, better targeting the governmental safety net at families in need of assistance, and redesigning some federal programs with no anti-poverty mission in a way that also meets anti-poverty objectives.

10. To better prepare for future downturns in the business cycle, policy makers need to modernize TANF (Temporary Assistance for Needy Families) and the Unemployment Insurance program and create an automatic link between the size of block grants to the states and trends in the business cycle. By making the governmental safety net act even more like an automatic stabilizer, policy makers can serve two key goals: boosting the economy *and* the well-being of low-income Americans.

More than anything else, what is needed is a rapidly growing economy that can boost sharply the levels of employment and earnings, especially in the bottom half of the income distribution. A more robust recovery will help the poor directly, but also indirectly, by easing fiscal pressures on households and governments, thereby stimulating philanthropic giving and reducing the temptations of politicians to cut spending for the safety net. Unfortunately, it is far easier to advocate a rapidly growing economy than it is to arrange one.

The book is organized as follows. Following this Introduction, Chapter 1 considers how recessions are defined and how the Great Recession of 2007–09 compares with previous recessions in the United States. The focus is labor market outcomes. Chapter 2 reviews some alternative definitions and measures of poverty, depicts the national trends in the rate of poverty, and presents the evidence that poverty continues to rise, even though the Great Recession "officially" ended in June 2009. This chapter also explores how poverty is trending in various states and among different demographic subgroups, and then consider forecasts of where the poverty rate may be headed between now and 2020 and the potential long-term effects of poverty on families and children. Chapter 3 considers how much private philanthropy in the United States is directed at the poor and how well charitable donations fared in the Great Recession. Chapter 4 evaluates the governmental safety net, particularly Unemployment Insurance, federal food assistance, federally supported cash assistance to adults with dependent children (both the disabled and non-disabled), the Earned Income Tax Credit, and federal housing assistance. The focus is how well the safety net worked during and after the Great Recession. Chapter 5 examines the role of the 2009 Recovery Act (often called the "federal stimulus package") and how it kept the unemployment rate from increasing even further and prevented many families from joining the ranks of the new poor. With the temporary stimulus package expired and fiscal pressures building at all levels of government, we show how low-income Americans are at risk of budgetary cutbacks, despite the economic recovery that has been underway since June 2009. The final chapter presents our suggestions for policy makers, both near-term (2013–2020), during the slow recovery to full employment, and long-term during future downturns and recoveries.

1
The Great Recession
Definition, Duration, and Impact

A recession is an overall slowdown in economic activity in a geographic region, as opposed to a slowdown in sales by a particular company or in a specific industry sector. The key measures of economic activity are Gross Domestic Product (GDP), income, employment, industrial production, and sales of goods at the wholesale and retail levels. The GDP is a measure of the overall value of goods and services produced by the economy. It is widely watched by market actors to determine whether the economy is expanding or shrinking.

Countries around the world vary in how a recession is defined and who is empowered to make the determination. In the United Kingdom, for example, recessions are generally defined by the government with a strict numeric definition: two consecutive quarters—or a total of six months—of negative growth in GDP constitutes a recession. The term "negative growth" means that the overall size of the economy is actually declining rather than increasing, as is typical of a healthy economy.

In the United States, the definition of recession has some degree of subjectivity because a committee of economists is tasked with determining whether there has been "a significant decline in economic activity spread across the economy, lasting more than a few months."[1] Since 1920, this determination has been made by the National Bureau of Economic Research (NBER), a private nonprofit research organization based in Cambridge, Massachusetts. The NBER "Business Cycle Dating Committee" looks at a variety of economic indicators (not GDP alone) and determines when a decline in economic activity occurred, whether it was "significant" (in severity), and—if a recession has occurred—when a recession ended. The number of months from when the economy began to decline (starting from its peak) to when the economy started to recover (the trough- its lowest point) is the duration of the recession.

According to the determinations of NBER, 17 recessions in the United States have occurred since World War I (see Table 1). They range in duration from six months (January to July 1980) to 43 months in the case of the Great Depression (August 1929 to March 1933).[2] When a recessionary economy reaches its trough and the next expansion begins, the economy usually expands for at least several years. There is only one case in modern U.S. history of a double-dip recession, meaning that the economy began to expand and then slipped back into recession (January 1980 to July 1980; July 1981 to November 1982). Some analysts refer to this period loosely as the recession of 1980–1982.

Changes in the unemployment rate, though watched closely by politicians as well as economists, are not used in defining when a recession begins and ends. When an economy is growing and is nearing its peak, the rate of decline in the unemployment rate actually tends to slow and the rate may even rise a bit, before the economy reaches its peak size (measured by GDP). At this stage of the business cycle, the unemployment rate is a "leading" indicator of where the economy is headed. On the other hand, the unemployment rate also acts as a "lagging" indicator when a recession ends because unemployment continues to rise after the official recovery has begun. Thus, the hardships induced by a recession, often measured by the amount and duration of unemployment, occur in the aftermath of the recession as well as during the official recessionary period.

In general terms, contractions in the modern U.S. economy appear to be related to one or more of six types of "shocks": oil prices, monetary policy, productivity, uncertainty, liquidity-financial risk, and fiscal policy. Recessions tend to be more severe when the economy is subjected to multiple shocks rather than only one.

Market analysts sometimes talk about "shocks" and the "business cycle," including peaks and troughs, as if it can be predicted

Table 1. U.S. Business Cycle Expansions and Contractions, 1920-2007. Contractions (recessions) start at the peak of a business cycle and end at the trough.

Business Cycle Reference Dates*		Duration in Months	
Peak	Trough	Expansion**	Contraction***
January 1920 (I)	July 1921 (III)	10	18
May 1923 (II)	July 1924 (III)	22	14
October 1926 (III)	November 1927 (IV)	27	13
August 1929 (III)	March 1933 (I)	21	43
May 1937 (II)	June 1938 (II)	50	13
February 1945 (I)	October 1945 (IV)	80	8
November 1948 (IV)	October 1949 (IV)	37	11
July 1953 (II)	May 1954 (II)	45	10
August 1957 (III)	April 1958 (II)	39	8
April 1960 (II)	February 1961 (I)	24	10
December 1969 (IV)	November 1970 (IV)	106	11
November 1973 (IV)	March 1975 (I)	36	16
January 1980 (I)	July 1980 (III)	58	6
July 1981 (III)	November 1982 (IV)	12	16
July 1990 (III)	March 1991(I)	92	8
March 2001 (I)	November 2001 (IV)	120	8
December 2007 (IV)	June 2009 (II)	73	18

* Quarterly dates are in parentheses
** Previous trough to this peak
*** Peak to trough

Source: Adapted from data available from the National Bureau of Economic Research (NBER), http://www.nber.org/cycles.html. Note that the NBER does not define a recession in terms of two consecutive quarters of decline in real GDP. Rather, a recession is a significant decline in economic activity spread across the economy, lasting more than a few months, normally visible in real GDP, real income, employment, industrial production, and wholesale-retail sales.

when recessions will begin and end. If anyone had such knowledge (and others did not), the informed individual could make a fortune in the stock market, since the average values of stocks are influenced by business cycles. Despite the many boastful claims that are made about economic forecasting, validated models that predict whether a recession will occur, and when it will begin and end, have remained elusive.[3]

Periods of contraction and recovery do not affect everyone equally. The pattern during the last three decades in the United States has been one of disproportionate hardships for men, blacks, Hispanics, younger workers, and less educated workers. Those recession-induced hardships are measured by changes in employment, hours of work, earnings, and income.[4]

Men, in particular, are more likely to be affected by changes in the labor market than are women. This is attributable largely to the fact that men are more likely than women to be employed in industries such as construction and manufacturing that typically slow down during a recession. Economists say that these industries are "cyclical" in nature. Women are more likely to be employed in less cyclical industries such as services and the public sector.

The Great Recession of 2007–2009

The United States recession that occurred from December 2007 through July 2009 was triggered by an initial spike in oil prices and a correction in housing prices, followed by a financial crisis, financial market disruptions, and prolonged uncertainty, in part due to policy uncertainty.[5] This period is called the "Great Recession" because it is the longest recession (18 months) since the Great Depression (43 months), much longer than the duration of the average recession (11 months) in the post–World War II period. As we shall see, the Great Recession is also unusual because of the extent of hardship that it caused in the United States, much more than in any downturn since the 1930s.

During the Great Depression, the unemployment rate in the United States surpassed 25 percent. By way of comparison, the unemployment rate more than doubled due to the Great Recession, from 4.5 percent in November 2007 to a peak of 10.6 percent in

January 2010, though it had declined to 8.2 percent by June 2012 and 7.8 percent in September 2012. Thus, the Great Recession—as harmful as it was—is not on par with the Great Depression in the scale of hardship that was inflicted. The recession of 1980–82 also saw unemployment exceed 10 percent, but the pace of recovery in job growth has been much slower in the aftermath of the Great Recession than it was after the 1980–82 recession. No other post–World War II recession comes close to matching the adverse job impacts of the Great Recession.[6]

A sluggish recovery of the U.S. economy, measured by GDP growth, has been underway since July 2009. The upturn seemed to accelerate somewhat in late 2011, but slowed down a bit in 2012 after a holiday burst. Although fears of a possible double dip recession rose and diminished several times during the post-2009 recovery, the overall pace of GDP growth has remained positive but below 3 percent per year, much too slow to generate a rapid fall in the unemployment rate.

Underemployment

A good overall indicator of the health of a country's labor market is the rate of underemployment, which is defined as the sum of the unemployment rate and the part-time employment rate (counting part-time workers who would like more hours of work). As an alternative to the official unemployment rate reported by U.S. federal government, since January 2010, Gallup has been publishing an underemployment measure based on daily national telephone surveys, including cell phones as well as landlines.[7] Gallup surveys a total of 30,000 Americans each month to track their employment situation.

The bad news is that the underemployment rate is much higher than the unemployment rate, estimated by Gallup at 17.5 percent in June 2012. This figure translates into about 20 million underemployed Americans. The June 2012 underemployment count was comprised of an 8.0 percent unemployment rate and a 9.5 percent rate of part-time work by employees seeking more hours of work.[8]

The good news is that the underemployment rate began trending downward in 2010 at a slightly stronger pace than the official unemployment rate. The underemployment rate was 19.5 percent in January 2010, rose briefly to 20.0 percent in April 2010 and then declined slowly to 19.0 percent in January 2011. Steady progress pushed the rate down to 17.8 percent in October 2011, but the rate rose again for four consecutive months to 19.1 percent in February 2012, before beginning to gradually decline again.

Long-Term Unemployment

The U.S. Bureau of Labor Statistics defines long-term unemployment as being unemployed for 27 weeks or longer, yet still looking for work. In some reports, 27 weeks is referred to as six months. When economic downturns occur, the absolute number of the long-term unemployed rises, as does the percentage of the unemployed who have been out of work for 27 weeks or more. High rates of long-term unemployment are a distinctive feature of the Great Recession.

Prior to the Great Recession, the number of long-term unemployed in the United States was fluctuating between 1.1 million and 1.3 million during 2006 and 2007. The count remained stable for the first five months of the Great Recession (December 2007 to April 2008), but then rose sharply to 1.6 million in June 2008, 2.6 million in December 2008, and 4.4 million in June 2009. Although the Great Recession ended in June 2009, the count of the long-term unemployed continued to rise to 6.1 million in December 2009 and to a peak of 6.7 million in June 2010.

The ensuing fall was due to a combination of improving economic conditions and a departure from the labor force of many discouraged job searchers. In any event, the count of long-term unemployed diminished rapidly for three months (to 6.1 million in September 2010). Yet it proceeded to rise again for three consecutive months (to 6.4 million in December 2010). There was no progress for the first eight months of 2011 but then, as if to bring some holiday cheer, the count dropped from 6.2 million in September 2011 to 5.6 million in December 2011. The first three months of 2012 showed a continued decline, but the trend reversed itself and rose to 5.4 million by June 2012.[9] Thus, according to the 27+ week definition, the count of long-term unemployed Americans increased by a factor of 5.6 from 2006 to mid-2010, with only a 20 percent decline in the count over the next two years.

Using a somewhat different measure (unemployment for a year or more), a study by Pew Charitable Trusts finds a similar pattern: The proportion of unemployed people who have been without a job for more than a year tripled from 9.5 percent in the first quarter of 2008 to 29.5 percent in the first quarter of 2012. In other words, in early 2012—almost 2.5 years after the official end of the Great Recession—nearly 13.3 million adults were jobless and looking for work, and 3.9 million of them had been looking for a year or longer.[10]

Bouts of unemployment became so long in the period after the Great Recession that the U.S. Department of Labor decided that they needed to change a key question on their major employment survey. Prior to January 2011, the "Current Population Survey" (CPS) did not allow respondents to indicate that they had been unemployed for longer than two years. If a respondent answered more than two years, the CPS coders put down two years in the official federal data file. Starting with January 2011, respondents were allowed to report unemployment durations up to five years. In future economic downturns, it will be feasible to track the frequency of very long bouts of unemployment and compare them to the very long bouts experienced after the Great Recession.[11] As we argue in the next chapter, long-term bouts of unemployment are tightly linked to poverty.

Young Adults' Employment Problems

Young adults, defined as people between the ages of 16 and 24, experience more employment difficulties in all phases of the business cycle—recoveries as well as downturns. On average, the youth unemployment rate is about twice as large as the unemployment rate for older working age adults. For example, in 2011 the youth unemployment rate was 17.3 percent; it was 7.9 percent for adults ages 25 through 54.[12]

The Great Recession hit young adults hard. In 2011, the youth unemployment rate hit 18.4 percent, the largest recorded rate since the statistic began to be tracked by the federal government in 1948.

The labor force participation rate declined from 59.4 percent in 2007 to 55.0 percent in 2011, at the same time that the unemployment rate among young adults climbed from 10.5 percent to 17.3 percent. In 2007, among blacks and Hispanics, the unemployment rate jumped from 19.3 percent and 10.7 percent, respectively, in 2007 to 29.0 percent and 19.4 percent, respectively.[13] Although the youth unemployment rate declined somewhat in 2011, no further progress was made in the first six months of 2012 until a slow decline resumed.

Youth unemployment has both an immediate and long-term impact on earnings. Studies that track young people over time find that a six-month spell of unemployment at age 22 is associated with, on average, an 8 percent lower wage rate one year later, a 5 percent lower wage rate by age 26, and a 2 to 3 percent wage loss by ages 30–31.[14]

Both high school graduates and college graduates have faced a very difficult job market during the slow recovery from the Great Recession. The unemployment rate for high school graduates under age 25 who are not enrolled in school was 22.5 percent in 2010. Among black high school graduates, it was 31.8 percent; among Hispanics it was 22.8 percent, and among whites it was 20.3 percent. The youth unemployment rates among college graduates not enrolled in school were 19.0 percent for blacks, 13.8 percent for Hispanics, and 8.4 percent for whites; 9.3 percent overall. All of these rates are much worse than what was recorded in the two previous U.S. recessions of 1990 and 2001.[15]

Even young adults who are employed are struggling in the aftermath of the Great Recession. Their average, inflation-adjusted weekly earnings declined 6 percent from 2007 to 2011, the largest drop in any age group of workers. Only 11 percent see their current job as part of a career, while 89 percent state that they are not making enough money to live the kind of life that they want to live.[16]

Although many young adults count on their parents to provide support in difficult times, the Great Recession also squeezed their parents in many ways—declining home values, higher rates of unemployment, lower wages, diminished value of investments, and tightened access to credit all limited many parents' abilities to help their offspring. While many young people pursue additional schooling when they can't find a good job, the resulting debt burden is substantial. In 2009, 56 percent of public university students graduated with an average debt of $20,467 while 65 percent of private university students graduated with an average debt of $26,728.[17] Not surprisingly, one in four young adults has moved back home after trying to live on their own.[18]

A possible increase in poverty among young adults is a growing concern among poverty scholars.[19] As we shall see in Chapter 4, young adults without children do not have much access to the governmental safety net. They lack enough job experience to benefit much from Unemployment Insurance. Cash welfare assistance at the state level is typically restricted to parents with young children. Food Stamps are an option, but can be received by able-bodied adults without children for only three months in a 36-month time period. The Earned Income Tax Credit is a significant plus, but only if a young adult has some earnings. Depending upon one's view, the Affordable Care Act will be a mixed blessing starting in 2014: It will compel many young adults to purchase health insurance, but it will also allow young adults with incomes less than 133 percent of the poverty line to enroll in Medicaid.

The Jobs-to-People Ratio

When unemployed people give up looking for jobs, they are no longer counted in the official unemployment rate. [20] To account for this so-called "discouraged worker" effect, it is useful to consider a different indicator: the ratio of employed people to the total number of working-age people in the U.S. economy. This "jobs-to-people" ratio is considered a valid measure of how well an economy creates jobs.[21]

In healthy economies, this ratio hovers in the range of 0.60 to 0.70. Prior to the Great Recession, this ratio was fairly stable in the United States, around 0.625 from January 2003 to January 2008. It then began to plummet in early 2009 to a trough of 0.582 in December 2009. The jobs-to-people ratio recovered little in the next two years, and was recorded at 0.585 in 2011 and 0.587 in September 2012.[22] These data suggest that the reported progress in reducing the unemployment rate may not be as encouraging as we thought, since increasing numbers of the unemployed may simply be giving up on the search for a job.[23]

If the jobs-to-people ratio is flat from one year to the next, it does not necessarily mean that the economy is not producing a net increase in jobs (see Table 2). What it means is that the net increase

Table 2. Jobs to People Ratio, by Month, January 2003 to June 2012, by Percent; Population 16 Years and Over

Yr/Mo	Jan	Feb	Mar	Apr	May	Jun	Jul	Aug	Sep	Oct	Nov	Dec
2003	62.5	62.5	62.4	62.4	62.3	62.3	62.1	62.1	62.0	62.1	62.3	62.2
2004	62.3	62.3	62.2	62.3	62.3	62.4	62.5	62.4	62.3	62.3	62.5	62.4
2005	62.4	62.4	62.4	62.7	62.8	62.7	62.8	62.9	62.8	62.8	62.7	62.8
2006	62.9	63.0	63.1	63.0	63.1	63.1	63.0	63.1	63.1	63.3	63.3	63.4
2007	63.3	63.3	63.3	63.0	63.0	63.0	62.9	62.7	62.9	62.7	62.9	62.7
2008	62.9	62.8	62.7	62.7	62.5	62.4	62.2	62.0	61.9	61.7	61.4	61.0
2009	60.6	60.3	59.9	59.8	59.6	59.4	59.3	59.1	58.7	58.5	58.5	58.2
2010	58.5	58.5	58.5	58.7	58.7	58.5	58.5	58.5	58.5	58.3	58.2	58.3
2011	58.4	58.4	58.5	58.4	58.4	58.2	58.2	58.3	58.4	58.4	58.5	58.5
2012	58.5	58.6	58.5	58.4	58.6	58.6	58.4	58.3	58.7			

Source: Bureau of Labor Statistics, U.S. Department of Labor, 2011, http://data.bls.gov/timeseries/LNS12300000.

in jobs has been cancelled by the net increase in the size of the U.S. adult population, which is growing slowly each year. In order for the jobs-to-people-ratio to rise, the economy needed to generate more than 150,000 net jobs per month, a rate that has not been consistently accomplished since the end of the Great Recession in June 2009. Three years after the recovery began, the U.S. economy was generating less than 100,000 jobs per month (May and June, 2012)[24], although somewhat more job creation (114,000) was reported in September 2012.

Looking Forward: Slow Recovery at Best

Private analysts forecast a continued decline in the unemployment rate in 2012 but at a slow pace.[25] The Federal Reserve Board forecasted rates of unemployment of 8.0 to 8.2 percent through the end of 2012, 7.5 percent to 8.0 percent at the end of 2013 and 7.0 to 7.7 percent at the end of 2014. However, the Fed acknowledged the possibility that the unemployment rate would not fall below 8 percent until the end of 2014.[26] For long-term budget forecasts, the U.S. Congressional Budget Office assumes the economy will not be at full employment (around 5 percent) until 2017.[27] Thus, many Americans could continue to experience economic hardship for some time to come.

The Boston Consulting Group argues that the U.S. economy cannot improve significantly without a stronger sense of optimism among consumers. Three years after the official end of the Great Recession, a survey of 1,500 people found that about four in ten Americans did not believe the economy would improve in the next several years. The number of people who plan to increase personal spending in the next year was equaled by the number of people who plan to curtail personal spending. Nearly half of respondents reported that they are not financially secure and almost a third reported that they have no savings whatsoever.[28]

Could the U.S. economy enter another recession, before full employment is reached again? Until the financial crises deepened in Europe, the consensus seemed to be that a double dip was unlikely. But the first six months of 2012 were challenging, to say the least, in Europe. By mid-2012, the unemployment rate in the 17-nation Euro zone had risen to 11.1 percent, the highest recorded rate since the Euro unemployment rate began to be counted in 1995.[29] Since the economies of Europe and the United States are highly interdependent, a U.S. recession could follow what appears to be a new recession in Europe.

The U.S. Congressional Budget Office (CBO) has forecasted another scenario leading to a U.S. recession in 2013. This scenario has less to do with Europe than a possible inability of U.S. fiscal policy makers to prevent an automatic tax increase in 2013 combined with a series of automatic spending cuts. Under this scenario, CBO projected a "mild recession" in the first half of 2013 followed by a slow recovery in the second half of 2013 and suggested that the rate of unemployment could actually rise again, perhaps to over 9.0 percent, by the end of 2013.[30]

Is it possible that the U.S. economy will never again see an unemployment rate below 5 percent? Although this is a sobering thought, most economists see few structural reasons for believing that a healthy recovery cannot bring the unemployment rate to the same low levels that were present in 2006–07. It may simply take the economy a long time to get there.[31] On the other hand, future economic downturns in the United States may be deeper and may have slower recoveries than was customary in the 1980–2007 period.[32] Since that may be a central lesson of the Great Recession for policy makers, we return in Chapter 6 to the question of how America's safety net can be strengthened to protect the poor in future downturns.

Regardless of the course economic recovery takes, low-income Americans remain at substantial risk. The risk is rooted in the slow pace of average monthly job creation, low wages, and the persistence of high rates and long bouts of unemployment and underemployment. The Great Recession may be over but its adverse effects on low-income Americans will continue and may worsen before they get better.

2

The Impact of the Great Recession on Poverty in the U.S.

We have established that the Great Recession caused a sharp increase in the U.S. unemployment rate, including the proportion who are unemployed long term. We turn now to the phenomenon of poverty and explore whether this metric of hardship has also been affected by the Great Recession.

Unfortunately, there is no universally agreed upon definition of "poverty." Defining who is "poor," particularly in a wealthy country like the United States, is challenging, both methodologically and philosophically.

For some, "poverty" conjures up images of malnourished children living in less developed nations. For others, the images may be of an historical nature, for example, bread lines, or the famous picture known as "Migrant Mother," of a poor woman, her children's heads buried in her shoulder, taken by Dorothea Lange during the Great Depression of the 1930s.

In this chapter, we explore the different ways in which poverty can be defined and measured, including how it is measured in Europe. We then consider the official U.S. measure of poverty that has been used for decades, what it does and does not capture, and what its shortcomings are. And we explore some alternative measures of poverty that are gaining some traction, even though they are not yet officially in use.

Regardless of which measure is used, we find that poverty is remarkably widespread, despite the obvious wealth of the U.S. Our principal objective is to understand how poverty trends, overall and in various subgroups, have been affected by the Great Recession. We present evidence that poverty continued to increase, well after the official end of the Great Recession in June 2009. Using the best evidence and forecasting models, we consider whether poverty has begun to decline, or how long it may be before poverty begins to decline. The chapter concludes with a brief discussion of the debate regarding the underlying causes of poverty, since the assumed causes often shape policy responses to poverty.

Measuring Poverty: An Overview

The United Nations, in its Millennium Development Goals initiative, defines poverty, in part as: (1) living on less than $1 per person per day; and (2) experiencing malnourishment, hunger, and/or very low weight.[33] However, using this definition—or even the World Bank's definition of living on less than $2 per person per day—is probably only broadly relevant for countries in places such as Africa, Southeast Asia, and Latin America, where incidences of hunger and very low income are still prevalent.

In general, the number of people in poverty (or the rate of poverty) in an advanced industrial country is calculated using either an *absolute* measure or a *relative* measure that is based upon an individual's or household's income. An absolute measure sets the poverty line at some fixed point, and families with incomes below that level are considered to be poor. A relative measure defines poverty relative to the standard of living within a particular country (e.g., relative to the median family). In practice, relative measures of poverty typically consider someone to be poor if his/her income is below some fraction of the country's median income (e.g., below 50 percent of median income). According to this method, the poverty threshold changes as the median income in the country changes.[34]

The U.S. uses an absolute measure, while many Western European countries use relative measures. The decision as to which measure to use is controversial. For example, an absolute measure set too low may not accurately reflect the challenges of residing in a country with a high cost of living. Few people might be counted as poor, yet many more might have difficulty covering basic needs such as housing payments. A relative poverty measure takes into account differences in standards of living across space and time by adjusting the poverty line as a nation's aggregate income increases (or decreases). However, it can be difficult to assess whether progress has been made in reducing poverty if the benchmark (e.g., below 50 percent median income) changes significantly over time.[35] If the overall income distribution of a country increases, median income rises, but so too does the income of those toward the bottom of the distribution. These individuals could in fact be better off, but a relative measure, which shifts with changes in overall income, would not reflect this change.

Both absolute and relative poverty measures typically are income-based, which also has limitations. In the U.S. and many European countries, poverty status is measured at a point in time, for example, by examining annual income. Yet, individuals and households may have other resources at their disposal such as assets (e.g., savings), access to credit, and the voluntary sharing of resources among extended family members. Drawing upon these resources may allow families to "smooth" their consumption over periods of time when income fluctuates. Some have argued that consumption, rather than income, is a better measure of an individual's or family's well-being. Rather than examining annual income, proponents of this approach typically quantify the value of the goods and services that the family consumes, usually by measuring their spending.[36] Some families who are officially recorded as "poor" (based on income measurement) may consume more goods and services (e.g., food, gasoline, air conditioning, refrigerators, and cars) than some people who are recorded as "non-poor."

Based on overall consumption patterns, certain analysts, most notably those at the Heritage Foundation, have argued that those classified as poor in the U.S. and other developed countries do not necessarily experience severe deprivation, since the overwhelming majority of the poor live in dwellings with refrigerators, televisions, microwaves, and air conditioning.[37] Of course, in a country like the U.S., one might expect all households to have, at the very least, refrigerators.

Finally, although not used in the U.S., the countries of the European Union (EU) have begun to use non-monetary indicators to measure what is commonly termed "social exclusion." Beyond lack of income, poverty may also entail lack of access to quality education and housing, poor health, and labor market discrimination.[38] Individuals who lack these opportunities or experience negative outcomes may not be able to participate fully in society and may face limited prospects for full integration.

Measuring Poverty in the U.S.: An Outdated Method?

As noted earlier, the U.S. uses an absolute measure of poverty; individuals or families whose pre-tax cash income falls below official poverty thresholds are considered "poor." The U.S. Census Bureau updates the poverty thresholds annually based on the average increase in cost of living in the United States, but otherwise the official measurement of poverty has remained the same since the 1960s. In 2010, a family of four (two non-elderly adults and two children) was considered poor if the family's total income fell below $22,113.[39]

The U.S. method of measuring poverty originated in the Johnson Administration's "War on Poverty." A statistician named Mollie Orshansky took the amount of money needed to afford a low-cost diet in 1955, multiplied that number by three (since at that time, the typical family spent approximately one-third of its income on food), and made adjustments based upon the number of related individuals in the household and the ages of those individuals (e.g., the elderly are assumed to need less food than younger adults and children).[40] The resulting figures are called the "poverty thresholds." In 1969, the Bureau of the Budget (now called the Office of Management and Budget [OMB]) required all departments and agencies of the executive branch of the federal government to use the Orshansky method, and OMB and Congress have used this method for almost half a century.[41]

The U.S. poverty thresholds have become widely used. For example, the thresholds and related guidelines are used by agencies such as the Department of Health and Human Services in setting eligibility criteria for a number of federal programs. Some programs use a multiple of the poverty thresholds, such as having income at or lower than 125 percent, 133 percent, 185 percent, 200 percent or 300 percent as part of criteria used to establish eligibility. While many federal assistance programs make some use of the poverty thresholds in determining eligibility, others do not.[42]

Despite its widespread use and longevity, many academics and policy makers have criticized the current method used in the United States. The data and assumptions underpinning the definition of the threshold are no longer accurate. Consumption patterns have changed dramatically since the late 1950s, but the poverty threshold does not reflect those changes.[43] Moreover, the threshold is the same whether a family resides in a large city or a small rural community and it is the same across the 48 contiguous states. In other words, the substantial variation in the cost of living between and within regions is not taken into account

The way that the Census Bureau calculates income is also problematic. In-kind benefits that enhance a family's ability to consume goods and services, such as Food Stamps (now called the Supplemental Nutrition Assistance Program, or SNAP, which limits families' out-of-pocket expenses for food), are *not* counted; nor is income from tax refunds, which provides a substantial benefit at tax time for many working families in the lower part of the income distribution. Also not accounted for are Social Security taxes subtracted from cash income, even though they reduce a family's disposable income.

In 1995, a panel convened by the U.S. National Academy of Sciences (NAS) proposed a series of recommendations to modernize how poverty is measured, including recalibrating the threshold to reflect current spending patterns on food, housing, clothing, and other basic expenses, and making adjustments for geographic variations in the cost of living. Although updated consumption data were used to refine the poverty threshold, the panel did not recommend use of a consumption-based measure of poverty. The panel did recommend an expansion in the sources of income counted when determining a family's money income. The panel also recommended that certain out-of-pocket expenses incurred by the family, in particular child care expenses, work-related transportation costs, and medical expenses, as well as payroll and income taxes, be subtracted from income before poverty thresholds are applied. However, the NAS proposal does not count in-kind benefits from Medicaid, Medicare, the federally funded health insurance programs, and other health-related government programs because they cannot be used to increase consumption of food, shelter, and other necessities.[44]

In 1999, the Census Bureau began to release a set of "experimental measures" of poverty that reflect the NAS recommendations. Some of these measures are variations on the official poverty calculus and hence represent absolute measures of poverty; those that employ the NAS poverty line represent a quasi-relative measure of poverty because the thresholds increase as consumption levels rise in non-poor families.[45]

In the fall of 2011, the Bureau released a "Supplemental Poverty Measure" (SPM).[46] The supplemental measure sets as the threshold the 33rd percentile of expenditures on food, clothing, shelter, and utilities for households with two children.[47] Adjustments are then made based upon family size and composition, but also for housing costs (i.e., whether the household is a renter, an owner with a mortgage, or an owner without a mortgage). Housing costs are allowed to vary by state of residence and by metropolitan area. This threshold would change over time to reflect changes in expenditures on food, clothing, shelter and utilities. On the income side of the poverty measure, the SPM goes beyond a count of pre-tax cash income. It counts the cash value of some in-kind benefits (e.g., federal food, housing, and energy assistance), subtracts income and payroll taxes, adds tax refunds, and subtracts necessary expenses for child care, work, and medical expenses (out-of-pocket only). Thus, the supplemental measure adopts the major recommendations of the NAS panel.

The SPM provides additional insight into the magnitude and distribution of poverty in America but it is not yet used by federal and state agencies in policy making or program administration.[48] For those purposes, the official measure of poverty, as designed in the mid-1960s, continues to be used with annual adjustments for inflation.

Poverty: Rates and Trends

Since some parts of the country began to experience the effects of the Great Recession in early 2007, before the official recession was declared in December 2007, we treat 2006 as the first full year prior to the onset of the Great Recession. In 2006, the real rate of GDP in the U.S. grew by a respectable 2.9 percent and the unemployment rate had recently fallen to 4.6, the lowest yearly rate since 2000. The shaded bars in Figure 1 represent "recessions," as officially recorded by the National Bureau of Economic Research (NBER).

Because recessions are associated with widespread job loss and loss of income, poverty tends to rise with recessions. Poverty rates tend not to fall until a year or more after the recession's official end, since it takes time for those who have lost jobs to find new employment (or higher paying employment).[49] In other words, even as the overall economy recovers, the poverty rate continues to rise for a variable period of time. The same pattern occurred after the Great Recession.

In 2010, according to the official Census Bureau definition, 46.2 million Americans were living in poverty, or 15.1 percent of the population. (The rate in 2011, 15.0 percent, was not statistically distinguisable from the 2010 rate.) The poverty rate using the SPM (Supplemental Poverty Measure) was slightly higher in 2010, about 16 percent. The 2010 poverty rate was the highest since 1993, although, as Figure 1 shows, the 2010 rate was still lower than the rate in 1959 (22.4 percent), the first year poverty was officially

Figure 1: Poverty Status of All People, 1960-2010.

Recession

Source: Authors' tabulations of U.S. Census data.

measured by the federal government. As Figure 1 indicates, the number of people living in poverty has increased each year since 2006, the year prior to the onset of the Great Recession: 36.5 million (2006), 37.3 million (2007), 39.8 million (2008), 43.6 million (2009), and 46.2 million (2010 and 2011). Between 2006 and 2010, the number of poor people grew by 27 percent while the total U.S. population grew by only 3.3 percent. Due to the severity and duration of the Great Recession and the slow recovery, it is projected that the poverty rate in the United States may continue to increase.[50]

Given the delays in publication of official U.S. poverty statistics, forecasting models have been built to project the poverty rate based on economic and other variables that are published more promptly.[51] For example, changes in monthly counts of SNAP (food stamp) recipients are a strong predictor of changes in poverty. Other economic variables such as the unemployment rate also predict near-term poverty trends.

Because SNAP serves individuals and families whose income is (generally speaking) at or below 130 percent of the poverty line, and because the program has a relatively high participation rate, when enrollments in SNAP are increasing, poverty is increasing; when enrollments in SNAP are declining, poverty is declining. (In Chapter 4 we explore whether SNAP and other income-transfer programs have cushioned the effects of the Great Recession on low-income families). This statistical association between SNAP enrollments and poverty is strong, even though some recipients of SNAP have incomes above the official poverty line. The point is not that SNAP enrollment is causing poverty but, as we shall see in Chapter 4, rising poverty boosts SNAP participation.

Monthly counts of SNAP recipients contain some good news and some bad news with respect to poverty trends. When the Great Recession ended in June 2009, there were 34.9 million Americans receiving SNAP. That figure grew steadily during the slow recovery to 39.0 million in December 2009, to 41.3 million in June 2010, to 44.1 million in December 2010, to 45.2 million in June 2011, and to 46.5 million in December 2011. In 2012, however, the march upward seems to have stopped. In fact, in January and February of 2012, the number of SNAP recipients actually declined slightly for two consecutive months to 46.3 million. This was the first two months of consecutive decline in enrollment since the period prior to the Great Recession.[52] However, SNAP enrollments climabed again to 46.7 million in July 2012, a new record.[53] Thus, if the trends in monthly SNAP usage maintain their correlation with poverty trends, poverty in America may not decline in 2012.

Based on forecasting models, poverty experts are expecting the Census Bureau to report further rises in poverty. According to one forecast, there will be almost 50 million Americans living in poverty by 2014, although this estimate was made before the significant decline in the unemployment rate reported at the end of 2011 and 2012.[54]

Poverty rates vary widely among subpopulations. Figure 2 shows the differences in poverty rates along racial and ethnic lines. Using the official measure, African Americans had the highest rate in 2010 (27.4 percent), followed by Hispanics (26.6 percent), Asian Americans (12.1 percent), and Whites (9.9 percent).).[55] The Supplemental Measure reports roughly similar patterns by race and ethnicity.[56] Since the onset of the Great Recession, the official

Figure 2. U.S. Poverty Rates, By Race: 1960-2010.

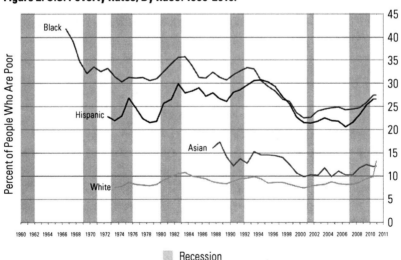

Source: Authors' tabulations of U.S. Census data.

poverty rate has grown faster among African Americans and Hispanics than among Asian Americans and Whites (see Figure 2).

The poverty rate also varies by age. Children are counted as poor if their families are poor. In 2011, children under 18 had the highest official poverty rate (21.9 percent), followed by persons 18 to 64 years old (13.7 percent), and persons 65 years and older (8.7 percent). Between 2007 and 2010 the poverty rate increased most dramatically among children under 18 (+4.6 percentage points), followed by persons 18 to 64 years old (+ 2.9 percentage points). Poverty decreased among persons 65 years and older during this time period (-0.4 of a percentage point).[57]

The share of poor children who are Hispanic is growing rapidly, in part due to the rapidly growing Hispanic population in the United States. From 2006 to 2010, the raw number of Hispanic children in poverty rose from 4.1 million to 6.1 million. The Hispanic share of poor children in 2010 was 37.3 percent, larger than the white share (30.5 percent) and the African American share (26.6 percent).[58]

The Supplemental Measure finds somewhat different poverty rates for the various age groups. In particular, there is somewhat less poverty among children and more among than elderly than the official measure reports. This difference is due primarily to the fact that the Supplemental Measure counts receipt of in-kind benefits such as SNAP as well as tax benefits that working poor families receive. Those adjustments lower the rate of childhood poverty. Moreover, the SPM subtracts out-of-pocket medical expenses from income, and this leads to a large increase in poverty among the elderly. The SPM poverty rate for children is 18.2 percent, while poverty rates among working-age adults and the elderly are 15.2 and 15.9 percent, respectively.[59]

National poverty trends mask large geographic variations in poverty. In 2010, the official poverty rate was highest in the South (16.9 percent), followed by the West (15.3 percent), the Midwest (13.9 percent), and the Northeast (12.8 percent).[60] The five states with the highest official poverty rates were Mississippi (22.7 percent), Louisiana (21.6 percent), Georgia (18.7 percent), New Mexico (18.6 percent), and Arizona (18.6 percent).[61] When the official measure and the SPM are used, a somewhat different group of states rank as the ten highest in terms of poverty rate. Under the official measure, eight of the ten states are in the South, and the other two are Arizona and New Mexico. The top ten under the Supplemental Measure include only five Southern states (including Florida, which is not in the top ten under the official measure), as the higher cost of living states of California, Hawaii, and New York enter the top ten. Five states appear in the top ten under both poverty measures: Mississippi, Arizona, Georgia, Texas, and Alabama (a complete ranking of the 50 states under each of the two poverty measures can be found online through the U.S. Census Bureau's website[62]).

In recent years, attention has been given to trends in "deep poverty," which is defined as living on income that is half (or less) of the poverty line for a given household size. For example, in 2010, a two-parent family with two children would be in "deep poverty" if their income fell below $11,157. The Census Bureau started recording rates of deep poverty in 1975, and in 2010 the rate of deep poverty was the highest ever since the figure was recorded: 6.7 percent.[63] However, the rate of deep poverty did not rise in 2011 (it actually declined slightly to 6.6 percent).

Although deep poverty appears to have been exacerbated by the Great Recession, one recent study argues that it has been rising steadily since 1983.[64] Moreover, there is some evidence that the Great Recession has brought about the kind of poverty—at least in terms of income—that is typically associated with developing countries. A recent analysis of national data finds that about 1.46 million U.S. households (or 18.4 percent of all poor households) were living on less than $2 per person per day, the World Bank's definition of extreme poverty, at some point during 2011.[65] This represents a 130-percent increase in the number of these households since 1996. Adding in the value of SNAP benefits to the calculation of income reduces the number of households in extreme poverty, but even so, 795,000 households would meet the $2 a day criteria. Within these households are 2.8 million (or 1.4 million adding in SNAP) children. While these numbers are small relative to the U.S. population as a whole (which was about 310.5 million in 2011), they do raise the question as to what sorts of supports could be provided to help alleviate poverty, deep poverty, and extreme poverty.

No Progress from 1980 to 2007?

Inspection of Figures 1 and Figure 2 suggests a distressing finding: The United States made no progress in reducing poverty from 1980 until 2007, despite the fact that the U.S. economy and the stock market took some of the largest strides upward in modern American history. Scholars are in disagreement about whether the finding is real and how to interpret these trends.

On one side of the debate, Robert Plotnick shows, using several different measures of poverty, that "since 1980 there has been little overall progress against poverty."[66] In addition to the official poverty measure, Plotnick explores a construct called "market poverty," which encompasses all forms of before-tax private cash income, including capital gains and the value of employer-provided health benefits. While the rate of market poverty is typically 45 to 55 percent higher than the official poverty rate and it rises and falls with the business cycle, there is no discernible trend since 1980.

Another measure, which Plotnick calls "adjusted poverty," tracks the official measure except (a) it adds income from capital gains and losses, the value of employer-provided health benefits, imputed income from home equity, certain tax credits on earned income, and government in-kind transfers for food, housing, and medical care and (b) it subtracts Social Security taxes and both federal and state income taxes. There was a slight decline in adjusted poverty from 1980 to 2007 but no sustained progress. Since the year 2000, the rate of adjusted poverty was about 30 percent lower than the official rate (because more sources of income are counted). Plotnick notes that adjusted poverty is similar to the NAS (1995) measure of poverty, except that NAS deducts some work expenses. The NAS measure also shows no progress since 1980.

Looking at subgroups, Plotnick finds that from 1980 to 2007 the poverty rate did decline for the elderly, blacks, and female-headed households, but it rose for children under the age of 18. This finding is not surprising, for several reasons: (1) Social Security benefits received by the elderly increase with increases in the cost of living, while some benefit levels of programs for families with children (e.g., cash welfare assistance) generally do not; (2) some programs that serve families with children have not grown since the 1970s, and in some periods faced retrenchment; and (3) less-educated individuals face a much different and less beneficial labor market.[67] The net effect, all groups combined, was no progress since 1980.

Plotnick also explores a measure of relative poverty, defined as half the median of either market income or adjusted income. Relative poverty is more than twice as large as the official rate of poverty, and it has been steadily increasing since the mid-1970s. This is another way of saying that income inequality has been growing since the mid-1970s.

Burkhauser and colleagues present a different interpretation. They argue that the definitions of income used in studies of the middle class may be too restrictive and explore a broader definition of income that is post–tax, post–transfers, and adjusted for family size. Although their focus is on progress in America's middle class, they also report results for low-income people. Their key result for the middle class is that real (inflation-adjusted) median income from 1979 to 2007 is up only 3.2 percent with a traditional measure, but is up 36.7 percent using the broadest measure of income. For the bottom quintile of the income distribution, income is down 33 percent using a traditional measure but up 26.4 percent using the broadest measure of income.[68] One of their key contentions is that the growing value of health insurance (not typically included in other measures of poverty and well-being) during this period should not be overlooked as a form of income that affects family well-being.

Bruce Meyer and James Sullivan, following the lead of others who are skeptical of standard poverty measures,[69] examined trends from 1980 through 2009 in three measures of well-being: a broad income measure that also accounts for errors in standard adjustments for inflation, a direct measure of consumption (on the theory that consumption reflects a family's expectation of permanent or averaged future income), and annual expenditures on housing and automobiles.[70]

With regard to income measures, they find that the tenth percentile of the pre-tax market income distribution rose by 30 percent from 1980 to 1999 but declined by more than 10 percent in the past decade. However, the tenth percentile of post-tax market income plus non-cash benefits rose steadily throughout the 1980–2009 period. Note that the tenth percentile of income is typically well below the official poverty line.

Perhaps their most striking result concerns average family consumption, defined as family spending (measured in dollars) on all goods and services. Those data come from a quarterly survey of 7,500 families from the first quarter of 1980 through the first quarter of 2010. They find that the tenth percentile of average family consumption, after correcting for inflation, rose 54 percent from 1980 to 2009. They construct a consumption-based measure of poverty that declines 75 percent from 1980 to 2009, causing them to conclude that there has been "substantial improvement in material well-being" among low-income families during this period.

As a robustness check, Meyer and Sullivan examine the quality of housing and automobiles in the bottom 20 percent of the income distribution from 1980 to 2009. They note that the bottom quintile includes some families with incomes above the official poverty line, but most of the families are below the official poverty line. Measured by square footage of housing space, presence of central air conditioning, dishwashers and clothes dryers, and absence of plumbing/roof leaks, they show clear evidence of housing improvement since 1980. With regard to automobiles, they looked at trends in car ownership rates and the fraction of cars with key features (air conditioning, power brakes, power steering, and other features). Once again, they report clear evidence of improvements since 1980.

Without trying to resolve the apparently conflicting ramifications of this body of research, we suggest that future studies should examine how the Great Recession has affected a wide range of poverty indicators in different regions of the country and in different subpopulations. Of particular interest will be how the "new poor," defined as families who entered official poverty due to the Great Recession, have been affected with respect to various indices of consumption as well as alternative measures of income and assets. Reliance on only one highly aggregated measure will not tell the complete story of the effects of the Great Recession on the poor, the near poor, and the new poor.

Employment and Poverty

It may seem obvious that unemployment can lead to poverty, but the magnitude of the relationship is remarkable. For individuals in families in which no one works, the poverty rate is nearly eight times as high as the poverty rate for individuals in families with at least one full-time, year-round worker (excluding those on Social Security). Over 75 percent of families with children that lack a full-time, year-round worker live in poverty.[71] Of course, some families have adults with physical or mental health or other problems that make it difficult to work, but the persistence of long-term unemployment is troubling because many families headed by the long-term unemployed will experience poverty, some for a substantial period of time.

The longer people are unemployed, the more difficult it becomes to obtain a job. Younger workers who lose their job and cannot find another job are blemished with a significant gap in their work history that can be difficult to overcome. Older workers with a solid earnings history who cannot find a job for a year or more may find it particularly hard to re-enter the labor force at a level of earnings near what they had previously accomplished. Not only are the skills of the long-term unemployed depreciating but they may become obsolete (since the jobs they had may be gone for good). Consequently, many of the long-term unemployed will be unable to find jobs in the same occupation they were in prior to the Great Recession.

A recent study examined parents age 25 to 54 who lost their jobs during the Great Recession or soon afterwards (May 2008 to February 2011). All parents in the study had at least three months of earnings followed by at least two months of unemployment. The authors found that the poverty rate for those who were out of work for six months or more at the end of the study was three times larger (35.3 percent versus 12.0 percent) compared to those with shorter bouts of unemployment. Of those experiencing long-term unemployment (six months or more), 69.8 percent received Unemployment Insurance compensation, but the average drop in income was dramatic: from $790 per month to $210 per month. Total monthly income from all sources dropped, on average, from $1,391 per month to $822 per month. The share of these families that ended up on SNAP doubled from 18.2 percent to 37.4 percent. Thus, the link between long-term unemployment and the probability of family poverty is real.[72]

Even as the recovery unfolds, many of the long-term unemployed may join the list of the "new poor." Their Unemployment Insurance (discussed further in Chapter 4) eventually expires. Without income from Unemployment Insurance, it is hard to imagine how a family escapes poverty without earnings. The combination of welfare (cash assistance) and SNAP (which is not counted in poverty rate calculation) will not bring a family to within 75 percent of the poverty line in all but three of the 50 states.[73]

As important as work is, it does not ensure that a family escapes poverty. The current federal minimum wage is $7.25, although about 18 states have enacted a higher minimum. If a worker makes $8 per hour, 35 hours per week for a year, the total earnings are $14,560. That is $2,145 under the official poverty level for a family of three. In other words, this family needs two workers to escape poverty or the lone worker needs to find a job with a higher hourly wage rate. In an economy with a 20 percent rate of underemployment, finding good-paying jobs is a major challenge, especially for workers who lack experience, education, and skills, or who have a checkered job history.

More research needs to be undertaken to determine how the Great Recession has influenced the duration of poverty spells. Prior to the Great Recession, the rule of thumb was that, among those who are poor, about 30 percent are poor less than a year and about 60 percent are poor for less than four years.[74] Of all those Americans who were not institutionalized yet experienced a bout of poverty from 1996 to 1999 (a prosperous period for the American economy as a whole), only about 2 percent were impoverished for all four years.[75] During the two-year period from 2009 to 2010, about 28 percent of the U.S. population had at least one spell of poverty lasting two months or more. Persistent poverty over the entire two-year period affected only 4.8 percent of Americans. Given that the Great Recession generated such long bouts of unemployment, researchers should explore whether the average duration of poverty has also lengthened, at least among non-disabled adults and among children in families led by non-disabled adults.

Poverty: Causes and Risk Factors

Our discussion of poverty thus far has implied that poverty is directly related to the performance of the economy: When the economy is booming, poverty rates are lower, whereas during recessions, poverty increases. While this relationship generally holds, this explanation does not account for why the overall poverty rates remain above 10 percent, even when unemployment has been quite low, and why certain groups, including children and people of color, experience higher rates of poverty.

The causes of poverty are multi-faceted and differ based on the circumstances of an individual or family. In general, spells of poverty begin because of changes in household composition (in particular, divorce or the birth of a child), job loss or not working at all, or disability.[76] Some of these causes, such as a disability, may be unavoidable, and job loss may be through no fault of one's own, while other changes may be more under the control of the individual (such as deciding to have a child when unmarried). Social scientists have developed a number of theories to explain the underlying phenomenon that drives poverty in the U.S. For simplicity's sake, we refer to them as "structural" and "behavioral" theories of poverty, even though behaviors may be induced by structural conditions and patterns or clusters of behaviors may exacerbate structural problems.

Structural Causes

A number of theories can be grouped together and thought of as structural in nature. The first is that changes in the structure of the economy can lead to poverty. These changes may be relatively short-term, or they may become permanent. A recession is a structural change; the economy contracts, jobs are lost, unemployment rises, and earnings from employment fall. Some subset of the jobless may fall into poverty as a result. Assuming the economy recovers and people return to work, the structural change may be temporary.

There may also be permanent changes in the functioning of the economy that are not related to the business cycle. The decline of manufacturing in the U.S. is an example of this type of structural change. In the years following the post–World War II boom, the manufacturing sector in the U.S. grew, along with the unionization of many of these jobs. As a result, individuals (mostly men) without a college education were able to obtain relatively well-paying, stable jobs with benefits that allowed them to support a family and achieve middle class status. Beginning in the 1970s, competition from other countries (e.g., Japan in the auto industry) and the outsourcing of factory work overseas resulted in fewer manufacturing jobs. Additionally, technological advances meant that the remaining work in the manufacturing sector required fewer hires, since much production was automated. Technological advances in other sectors meant that to secure a good-paying job, more education was required. The high school graduate who, in the 1960s might have found a secure and good-wage job, was now increasingly relegated to jobs in the service sector, where wages are low, benefits are few, and the risk of becoming poor is greater.[77]

Structural causes of poverty can also include a set of factors that sociologists call "social structures." Social structures refer to the ways in which positions, roles, and relationships are arranged within a particular institution, such as the economy.[78] Consider the United States' complicated relationship with race. Even after the repeal of slavery, Jim Crow laws in the South, discriminatory practices such as "redlining"(denying home loans to individuals living in predominantly minority neighborhoods), and school segregation, there and elsewhere, kept African Americans relegated to the bottom of the social hierarchy, denying many the opportunities to move ahead economically. Thus, this explanation contends, discrimination played a significant role in the extremely high poverty rates experienced by African Americans in the early 1960s, when official records first began to be kept.

While incidents of overt discrimination occur less frequently today, racial segregation in living patterns continues, and court decisions in the post–Civil Rights era have rendered public schools today more segregated than they were at the time the landmark of *Brown v. Board of Education* school desegregation case. Moreover, compared to whites, minority children are more likely to attend schools that are located in the central cities, where a variety of problems are prevalent: less experienced teachers, a majority of students coming from poor families, and elevated rates of crime and drug use. All of these factors are associated with lower achievement and graduation rates.[79]

The differences in educational experience, then, relegate minorities to schools that are inferior, and put children attending them at an elevated risk for poverty as adults (since they do not acquire the skills necessary to compete successfully in the labor market).

Changes in the economic and social structure can interact to affect the poverty rate, both positively and negatively. As the Civil Rights movement gained momentum and laws and court decisions barred certain types of discrimination, African Americans did gain access to jobs that had previously been off-limits, including unionized factory positions that provided decent wages and lifted some out of poverty while protecting others from falling into poverty. However, in the 1970s and 1980s, many companies producing goods in the U.S. (i.e., those that did not move production overseas) moved out of the central cities, where large numbers of African Americans lived, to the suburbs, making it more difficult for some African Americans to retain those jobs and potentially causing some families to become poor when adults lost jobs and/or could not find new ones.[80]

Behavioral Explanations

In contrast to structural explanations, which place emphasis on larger, societal forces, behavioral explanations of poverty tend to focus on individual and group behaviors as the cause of poverty. Some behavioral theories use structural causes as the starting point, others point toward individual shortcomings, while still others use the language of incentives and rationality to explain how certain behaviors encourage and perpetuate poverty. In general, the behaviors are non-work, reliance on public assistance, non-marital childbearing, criminality, and, for children, delinquency, failure to attend or complete school, and teenage pregnancy.

The phrase "the culture of poverty" has often been invoked as a shorthand for this set of behaviors. First proposed by anthropologist Oscar Lewis and based upon his observations of the poor in Mexico and Puerto Rico, the culture of poverty theory argues that when families and individuals experience long-term poverty, they develop feelings of defeatism, marginalization, helplessness, and dependency, which then leads to idleness, delinquency, criminal activity, prostitution, and other behaviors far outside mainstream culture.[81] Lewis traced the origins of this "culture" to structural changes in economic conditions, which left some subset of people poor and unable to participate fully in the resulting new economy. In response to their exclusion, the aforementioned behaviors develop, which are then passed on to the next generation, making it unlikely that the children and grandchildren of the poor will be able to escape poverty. Lewis also argued that these behaviors become so entrenched that even if economic conditions change, the values and behaviors of the poor remain, leading to a continued cycle of poverty.

After falling out of favor due to a concern that this explanation of poverty constituted "victim blaming" (that is, blaming the poor for causing their poverty), culture-based theories regarding poverty gained traction again in the 1980s and early 1990s. Contrary to structural theories, Lawrence Mead argues that poverty is simply a problem caused by lack of work or too little work effort, rather than few available jobs or a changing economy. Increasingly, Mead contends, the poor have been reluctant to take jobs they considered unacceptable, (e.g., low pay, bad working conditions) in large part because they lack a commitment to work, a characteristic he believes is central to mainstream American values. The only way to make certain the poor would work, he argues, is through compulsion.[82]

Charles Murray takes a slightly different tack, but arrives at the same conclusion—that poverty is the result of an unwillingness of the poor to work and to marry. Rather than a lack of commitment to the work ethic, Murray argues that the poor are merely responding to the incentives embedded within the U.S. public welfare system. Prior to reforms enacted in the mid-1990s, a poor family, says Murray, would be better off financially receiving public assistance than working in a low-wage job. Since public assistance rules favored single parents over married parents, a couple with children would need to remain unmarried to receive benefits.[83] Although Murray's argument does not posit that the poor are necessarily different in their values and orientation (he presumes that they are rational actors attempting to maximize income), he does pinpoint the cause of poverty on behavior.

A related rational-choice explanation for poverty is the flow of unskilled immigrants (undocumented as well as documented) into the United States. The immigrant population of the United States has nearly quadrupled since 1970 and doubled since 1990, although the patterns of immigrant assimilation into American society (e.g., learning English, voting) are uneven.[84] From the perspective of migrants from Mexico, for example, it may be perfectly reasonable for families to see life in the United States as more attractive than life in Mexico. Adult immigrants may have more job opportunities in the U.S. than Mexico and they may perceive the public schools to be better than what Mexico offers children. When unskilled immigrants arrive in the U.S. (perhaps without their families at first), the low-wage jobs that they occupy may not be sufficient to escape poverty by U.S. standards, even though the low-wage U.S. jobs are an improvement compared to wages in Mexico.[85] Due to the Great Recession, however, the pace of immigration into the U.S. has temporarily come to a virtual halt.[86] The slow recovery will eventually cause the flow immigration to resume again, absent major changes to immigration policy.

Once living in the U.S., it may take immigrants a period of time to escape poverty since their English skills may be inadequate for obtaining better-paying jobs, they have few connections, and their vocational skills may be limited. While some may first live in large cities, over time they follow employment opportunity, which is one of the explanations for the rise of suburban poverty in America.[87] There is strong evidence that poverty rates among immigrants groups decline quickly over time, and with only small adverse effects on the wages of low-skilled natives.[88]

Thus, it should not be surprising that the large flow of immigrants into the United States contributes, at any point in time, to a sizeable fraction of the measured poverty. However, while immigrants to the U.S. experience much higher rates of poverty than U.S. natives, many immigrants and their families escape poverty after a period of adjustment.

Structure or Behavior?
The Case of Single-Parent Families

While some pundits fall firmly within either the structural or behavioral camps, sorting out potential structural versus behavioral causes of poverty is quite difficult in practice. The case of poverty and family structure provides a good illustration of why this is so.

Family structure—that is, the composition of a family—has long been central to discussions about the causes and consequences of poverty. In good economic times and bad, poverty rates among households headed by a single mother with children under the age of 18 are much higher than those of married couples with children. Even when poverty rates among female-headed households were at record lows (around 33 percent in the early 2000s), the comparable poverty rate for married couple households was around 5 percent. While poverty rates among married couple families with minor children increased to 8.8 percent, up from 6.4 percent in 2006, the corresponding poverty rates for their single mother counterparts were 36.5 percent in 2006 and 40.7 percent in 2010. Poverty rates for families headed by single fathers are also relatively high: 24.2 percent in 2010. In relative frequency, however, the number of single father households is quite low.

If relatively few children lived in households headed by single mothers, concerns over these very high poverty rates might not be so great. But over time, more children spend at least some of their childhood with a single parent. In 1972, 12.8 percent of children resided in single mother households; by 2002, that figure was 22.8 percent; in 2011 that proportion was 23.6 percent.[89] African American children are more likely to live with a single mother (51.2 percent), and the poverty rate for African American single mother families in 2010 was 41.7 percent.

Whether single motherhood causes poverty or poverty contributed to that family structure is a question that is difficult to answer (one cannot randomly assign family types to test this question experimentally). The association between single mother families and poverty is certainly strong. The question, then, that many scholars and policy makers have asked is, why has there been such an increase in this type of family? Is it due to structural reasons or because of behavior?

One reason that poverty rates are lower among married couple families is that marriage often means two incomes. So why would a single mother not marry? When Wilson was conducting his work on the structural causes of poverty, particularly among African Americans in central cities, he coined the term "lack of marriageable men" to explain the phenomenon of single parenthood.

Structural changes in the economy did not just hamper low-skilled men's job prospects, but their marriage prospects as well. Poor women, he argued, had little incentive to marry the men with whom they had children, since these men lacked stable earnings to support a family. Rapid increases in incarceration in the 1990s and 2000s may also contribute to the problem. Prisoners, who are disproportionately male, less educated, and low-income,[90] may make poor spouses both when they are locked up and after release, when they face enormous challenges in securing employment.[91]

Even accepting that the pool of men available as partners to poor women is limited,[92] why have children outside of marriage if the risk of poverty is greater? Whereas the majority of single mothers in the 1960s were single due to divorce, children are increasingly being born to parents who are not married and who do not marry. The proportion of births that occur to unmarried women has been steadily rising, from 28 percent of all births in 1990 to 41 percent of births in 2008.[93] Some of those espousing behavioral causes of poverty might argue that the poor simply do not value marriage. However, survey and other data find that poor women (and men) place a high value on the institution of marriage and aspire someday to be married.[94] Additionally, while poor women are more likely than non-poor women to have children outside of marriage, the increased rate of non-marital childbearing also reflects larger, secular changes in society, including less stigmatization of single parenthood. As noted earlier, Murray argued that the availability of and rules surrounding public assistance benefits served as a deterrent to marriage among poor couples. Overall, though, research has found little to no effect of welfare policies on childbearing or marriage decisions.[95]

In the end, structural reasons may play a role for women as well. Like their male counterparts, less educated young women, both those who are poor or near poor, face limited economic prospects. While the unemployment rate for women with a high school degree or less was lower than it was for men in 2010 (14.6 percent versus 15 percent),[96] available jobs are likely to be low-paying and unlikely to lead to career advancement. For some of these women, having children may be a way to find meaning in their lives.[97]

The Effects of Poverty on Families and Children

Regardless of what one believes to be the causes of poverty, there are reasons to be concerned about the plight of the poor, even in a rich country like the U.S. Families who are poor or near poor are more likely than the non-poor to experience a variety of material hardships.[98] These include disruptions in housing through eviction or doubling up with others, disconnection of telephones and utilities, going without needed medical or dental care due to cost reasons, and changing eating habits or running out of food without the money to purchase more. Poverty also can have negative effects on adults' health. Poor adults are more likely to have serious health problems and to have higher mortality rates than non-poor adults.[99] However, it is the effects of poverty on children that may be of the most concern.

A large body of literature has established a strong association between experiencing poverty in childhood and a variety of outcomes in life, none of which are positive. Infant mortality and low birth weight are more common among poor children. Compared to children who are not poor, poor children are more likely to be in fair or poor health and to have more hospitalizations. In school, poor kids are much more likely to repeat a grade, be suspended or expelled, and/or drop out of high school. Teenage girls who are poor are more likely to have an unmarried birth, and as young adults, children who were poor are more likely to be out of school but not employed.[100]

The possible reasons for these disparities are many, including lack of income to purchase adequate health care and to live in good school districts, lack of preparation to attend school, and experiences of harsh parenting due to high stress levels of parents. More recent research on brain development has posited that stress brought on by poverty is experienced in utero, which can have lasting, negative effects for children.[101]

Now that data are available from longitudinal studies following children for very long periods of time, the long-term effects of childhood poverty are being seen. A recent study found that experiencing poverty between birth and age five is associated with lower earnings and fewer hours worked as an adult, even at ages as high as 37.[102]

Demonstrating statistical associations between poverty and adverse outcomes is much easier than demonstrating valid causal relationships, although some of the most recent research employs very sophisticated techniques in an attempt to do so. What is seen as an effect of poverty, for example, may be—at least in part—the effect of a correlated variable such as a low level of educational attainment among parents or low social status. In some cases, the causation may work in reverse (e.g., chronic health conditions may cause poverty). However, a series of experimental studies have demonstrated that boosts to family income, through earnings supplements similar to the EITC (Earned Income Tax Credit, discussed below), have been shown to improve children's academic performance, and in some cases, behavioral outcomes, although the evidence for adolescents is less encouraging.[103]

Children, as social scientists Jeanne Brooks-Gunn and Greg Duncan note, cannot avoid poverty if their parents are poor, nor can they do much to alter their family's circumstances—they cannot work, or if they can, their hours are limited. However, anti-poverty initiatives, whether operated through philanthropic efforts or public programs, could intervene to mitigate not only the immediate harmful effects of poverty on children, but also potential longer-term consequences

3

Philanthropy and America's Poor

Should poverty—the lack of resources to meet basic needs—be addressed by private charity or by the state? Or by both? Although most western European nations have substantial government-funded programs to help the poor, until recently, many Asian societies relied almost entirely upon family networks to support needy adults and children.[104] Today the U.S. relies on both private and governmental support but, as we shall see, that has not always been the case. In this chapter and the next we examine the systems of private and governmental support that comprise America's safety net. We focus on how well the systems responded to the brutal forces of the Great Recession.

The set of programs serving vulnerable, low-income people (the poor and near poor) is sometimes referred to loosely as the "safety net." However, there is some variation in the literature as to whether the safety net refers only to governmental programs or whether it also includes the combination of private, voluntary support of the poor (e.g., by family, friends, churches, charities, and community foundations). While there is no right answer to this matter of definition, we prefer to reserve the term "safety net" to mean the "governmental safety net" (federal, state, and local governments), in part because we do not wish to convey the impression that private and governmental supports for the poor are fused together in a well-coordinated "net" or even that the interaction of the two systems of support are adequately understood. Remarkably little is known about how much poverty is eradicated or attenuated by the large amounts of philanthropic donations made in the United States on an annual basis.

In this chapter our focus is on understanding the extent to which philanthropy directly serves the basic needs of low-income people, as opposed to buttressing specific sectors of society (e.g., the arts, medicine, and higher education) that will benefit virtually all citizens (including the poor). For human service programs that serve low-income populations and are supported—at least in part—by philanthropy, we seek to determine how well they have fared during the Great Recession and the slow recovery.

On the one hand, one might expect that philanthropists—from the ordinary church giver to the billionaire giver—would be most generous in times of great need, such as the Great Recession. On the other hand, economic downturns—particularly those that cause rapid reductions in the income and assets of citizens—also reduce the amount of money available for giving. The net effect of these two forces—an enhanced will to give but a diminished ability to do so—can be observed in the overall trends in philanthropic giving.

Before we consider the role of modern philanthropic activity in America's anti-poverty efforts, we take a brief detour to sixteenth-century England, where Queen Elizabeth I and the Parliament made a crucial decision: Can the needs of the poor in England be addressed adequately through charity alone, or does the state also need to play a key role? The Queen's responses to this question, including the related public debates, shape much of the public debate about the U.S. anti-poverty system.

The Elizabethan Poor Laws

Prior to the Reformation, the Christian duty, as described in Matthew chapter 25, was understood to be to feed the hungry, give drink to the thirsty, welcome the stranger, clothe the naked, visit the sick, visit the prisoner, and bury the dead. The instructions were clear, but they were not always followed. [105]

In fact, economic change in sixteenth-century England put great pressure on traditional approaches to community problem-solving.

During the reign of Elizabeth I the population of England rose from three to four million, a byproduct of both rising fertility and declining death rates. Wage controls for skilled workers were enacted to curb inflation, while a series of poor harvests contributed to rising food prices. A process of land enclosure favored less labor-intensive, large farms and rearing of sheep (for profitable wool trading) over traditional farming by individual peasant families. As a result, many rural families were evicted from their homes or voluntarily sought a better life in English towns and cities such as London and Norwich.

Historically, a town might have relied on a private benefactor who had left money in his will for an almshouse to provide shelter for the poor. But the swelling number of homeless and unemployed peasants overwhelmed the English towns, creating what was perceived as a serious threat to law and order. Vagabonds and beggars were disturbing community life.

The English Parliament responded with a series of laws in 1563, 1572, 1576, 1597 and 1601, referred to loosely as the Elizabethan "Poor Laws." They drew a sharp distinction between the "deserving poor" (children, the elderly, the sick, and families in need of temporary assistance due to unemployment), and the "undeserving poor" (e.g., pickpockets, beggars, and armed highwaymen), who were handled harshly, especially upon repeated offenses. For example, vagabonds were whipped or burned through the right ear—or even executed.

A national poor tax was introduced in 1572, compelling all citizens to pay for anti-poverty activities under threat of state punishment of those who did not pay. In 1576 each town was also required to provide work for the unemployed, thereby allowing the poor to perform a service for the community. And in 1597 each parish was required to appoint an official responsible for supervising the parish's response to the needs of the poor.

The Poor Laws signaled progression from an exclusive reliance on private charity to a combination of private charity and a welfare state with local implementation of national legislation. And this is the anti-poverty system that colonists would bring from England in the seventeenth century to America. However, it was not until the 1930s, when the U.S. was faced with the Great Depression, that the federal government developed a comprehensive welfare state. Prior to that, local charities and relief agencies, funded by philanthropic donations, were primarily responsible for dealing with the poor in their communities.[106]

The Non-Profit Sector

When we use the phrase "private charity," we are referring to non-profit organizations operating independent of government that are providing some form of assistance to low-income people. Sometimes that assistance may be in-kind, such as food provided by food pantries and soup kitchens, while other times the assistance may be service-based, such as assistance preparing a résumé and finding a job.

The terms "non-profit" and "charity" are not necessarily synonymous, though. The non-profit, or voluntary, sector in the United States is extraordinarily large and diverse. In 2009, more than 1.4 million organizations were registered with the Internal Revenue Service as 503(c)(3), the agency's designation for organizations that are tax-exempt because they do not turn profits. These organizations range from large hospitals and universities to smaller organizations providing direct services to the poor.[107] Within the category of "human services," the type of non-profit most likely to serve low-income individuals, great variation exists. Large, national organizations such as the Salvation Army, United Way, and Habitat for Humanity fall under this umbrella, as do locally based food pantries and homeless shelters.

While the focus of this chapter is on charitable giving, it is important to note that the budgets of non-profits providing human (and other) services are made up of a mix of private and public funds, and sometimes public funds are dominant. In 2010, approximately 33,000 non-profits throughout the country held government contracts and grants to provide some of their services, and for 62 percent of those, government funding accounted for a larger share of the budget than private funding.[108] For example, many non-profit agencies across the country operate the Head Start program, a federally funded early childhood development program for poor children. In the absence of federal Head Start dollars, it is unlikely that these non-profits would be able to provide a similar service. During economic downturns, though, those contracts may be at risk for cuts, as governmental revenues shrink, making funding received via charitable contributions all the more important.

Counting Charitable Gifts

Americans are givers. In calendar year 2011, the total value of charitable donations in the United States was estimated at just under $300 billion ($298.4 billion). There is no other country in the world that comes close to this magnitude of charitable giving. The overall giving figure represents an estimate of the donations made by 75 million households across the United States, more than 1 million corporations, an estimated 120,000 estates, and 77,000 foundations. Donations are awarded to more than 1.2 million IRS-registered charities and an estimated additional 350,000 American religious congregations.[109]

The $300 billion figure is based on an annual report, *Giving USA*, prepared by the Center on Philanthropy at Indiana University. The most important raw data are claims of charitable deductions on tax returns submitted by individual and corporate taxpayers to the Internal Revenue Service. Since final IRS data are not released until two years after the close of a tax year, the Center on Philanthropy has begun to utilize preliminary estimates of giving from the IRS, with updates and corrections made later when the final IRS data are available. Moreover, econometric models are utilized to compensate for the lack of comprehensive and timely IRS information. Those models build on studies showing how giving is correlated with well-measured economic indicators (e.g., total household consumption, tax rates, and the stock market) that are released on a prompt and regular basis. The models play a key role in estimating donations to specific sectors such as religious organizations.

Not all philanthropic activity is included in the $300 billion figure. For example, suppose a head of a household loses his or her job and does not have enough money to feed his or her immediate family. Relatives, friends, or neighbors may contribute cash, food, or clothing to help the troubled family meet its basic needs. Young adults who are in school or who cannot find a job may also receive support from their parents. According to a recent survey, more than one in ten American adults regularly receive money or financial assistance from their parents or other family members, with adults ages 18–24 most likely to receive money.[110] This important source of support is not counted in the $300 billion figure because the recipient, whether an individual or a family, is not a recognized charity and thus the donor is not permitted to claim a tax deduction for the assistance. Moreover, the $300 billion figure excludes the volunteer time that citizens devote to organizations such as Habitat for Humanity and the local soup kitchen. Volunteer time is not covered by the IRS charitable deduction.

While the $300 billion figure does not count all philanthropy, it certainly seems like a lot of money. If it were well spent, isn't it enough to eliminate or drastically reduce the incidence of poverty in America? For example, if we divide $300 billion by the Census Bureau's estimate of the number of poor people in America (just under 50 million in 2011), the quotient is $6,000 per person in poverty.

Unfortunately, $6,000 is not enough to support a person who has no other sources of income. Is it enough, though, to fill the average "poverty gap" in the United States, where the gap is defined as the average amount of additional income that a poor person needs to escape poverty (since most poor people do have some sources of income)? For persons with incomes near the poverty line, $6,000 of additional income may well be sufficient. But for the very poor, with incomes less than 50 percent of the poverty line, $6,000, while a big plus, is not enough to escape poverty. The Census Bureau estimates that in 2010, approximately 6.2 million families needed $5,000 or more to escape poverty, while about three million families could be lifted out of poverty with an additional $5,000 or less.[111] But there is a bigger problem with this line of reasoning. The $300 billion donated in 2011 does not go directly into poor people's pockets, but rather to services. Even more important, the $300 billion is not aimed entirely or even primarily at the poor (or even at low-income people living near or below the poverty line).

Giving in 1910 Versus 2010

A recent analysis of philanthropic giving in the United States compared the recipients of charitable donations in 1910 to the recipients of charitable donations in 2010. While the total volume of giving mushroomed from $163 million to almost $300 billion (in dollars unadjusted for inflation), the rough distribution of recipients suggests that some of the basic preferences of U.S. donors have been consistent for a century.

The largest single category of recipient is religious organizations (churches). Other popular targets of giving include educational organizations, art museums, parks, and hospitals. In 1910 there were also some large human service organizations that accounted for a significant share of donations (e.g., the Salvation Army, Red Cross, and the YMCA), as there are today. The focus of the largest 300 gifts in 2010 is quite instructive. Most went to colleges, universities, hospitals, medical centers, arts institutes, and an occasional advocacy organization. Only five of the 300 large gifts went to organizations that deliver services to people in communities. Looking at the basic patterns of giving, the analyst concluded that it seems likely that low-income populations, while they may benefit—indirectly as well as directly—from much of this giving, were not the primary target of a majority of the charitable gifts made in 1910 or in 2010.[112]

Patterns of Giving and Receiving in 2011

If we look at the most recent *Giving USA* report, which covers charitable donations in 2011, we find a similar pattern of giving behavior, despite the fact that poverty in America is at its all-time high mark and the rate of long-term joblessness is not expected to return to normal levels until the end of the decade. Here are the basic facts about U.S. charitable giving in 2011.

The primary givers in the United States are individuals, not corporations or large foundations. About 88 percent of the charitable donations in 2011 were made by individuals. Gifts from live individuals were flat but gifts from bequests were up 8 percent in 2011 over 2010. Corporate gifts are strongly influenced by in-kind awards, particularly by companies in the pharmaceutical sector.

Affluent individuals are increasingly putting their money into "donor-advised" funds that rely on professionals to help allocate gifts and allow pooling of gifts from multiple donors. The three largest donor-advised funds had an average increase in donations of 77 percent over 2010, even though overall giving in the U.S. was only slightly higher in 2011 than it was in 2010.

One of the challenges in philanthropy research is to define meaningful categories of the recipients of donations. The *Giving*

USA annual report covers donations to religious, educational, community foundation, human service, health, arts/culture/humanities, international, and environmental organizations. About 3 percent of the gifts do not seem to fit any of these categories. Here are the basic facts about the recipients (see Figure 3).

Religious organizations captured about 32 percent of total charitable giving in the United States, or close to $96 billion in 2011. Note that these gifts constitute part of the revenue flows that churches need to run their basic operations (pay the pastor, maintain the church building, and so forth). A gift to a church does not necessarily mean that a basic need for a poor person will be met.

Educational organizations (including colleges and universities) captured 13 percent of the gifts, or $38.9 billion. Some of this money supports scholarships for students from low-income families (though merit-based scholarships may be more common),

Figure 3. 2011 Contributions: $294.42 Billion by Type of Recipient Organization (in billions of dollars, all figures are rounded).

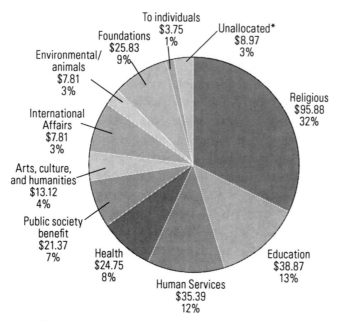

*Includes gifts to non-grantmaking foundations, deductions carried over, contributions to organizations not clssified in a subsector, and other unallocated contributions.

but much more of the money supports the basic research and teaching operations of schools, colleges, and universities, including support for athletic programs and facilities.

Private, community, and operating foundations received 9 percent of the total, or about $25.83 billion. The community foundations in particular may be a source of funds for service organizations that help low-income families. Direct giving to human service organizations accounted for 12 percent of the total, or $35.39 billion. This is the third-largest proportion of charitable dollars in 2011, and the same proportion of gifts received as in 2010. Health organizations received 8 percent of the total, or about $24.75 billion. However, some of the donations counted under "education" may go to research or teaching at medical schools. Seven percent, or $21.37 billion, went to public-society benefit organizations. (Giving categorized as "public-society benefit" includes gifts to organizations concerned with community organizing, civil rights, and civil liberties, as well as gifts to United Way, Jewish Federation, and combined funds, such as the Combined Federal Campaign.) Arts, culture, and humanities organizations captured $13.12 billion, or 4 percent of the total.

International affairs (relief, development, and public policy efforts) account for 8 percent of donations, or $22.68 billion. Environmental/animal organizations received 3 percent of the donations, or $7.81 billion. American charities that conduct development and relief work overseas were the only type of nonprofit group to experience giving that outpaced inflation by a significant percentage, at 4.4 percent, while donations to environmental causes increased by 1.4 percent after inflation. Giving to every other type of organization was either flat or declined. Among all these types of groups, religious organizations suffered the biggest drop, with donations falling nearly 5 percent, in part because of a decline in the number of Americans who belong to churches, synagogues, or mosques.

There is no way of knowing how much poverty in America will be affected by the $300 billion in donations made in 2011. In early 2007, however, before the onset of the Great Recession, IU's Center on Philanthropy collaborated with Google in a specialized study to determine how much of charitable giving by households in the United States was focused on the needs of low-income Americans.

Using 2005 giving data, they estimated that less than a third of charitable donations made by individuals were directed at the economically disadvantaged (poor and near poor). And only 8 percent of individual donations were reported as contributions to meet the basic needs of the poor (food, shelter, and other necessities). If all sources of donations are included (corporations and foundations as well as individuals), about 23 percent of private philanthropy went to programs specifically intended to help people of low income. Thus, the best available study—though it is not recent and has limitations—suggests that we should not expect any more than $0.25 on the dollar of charitable giving to be directly serving the needs of low-income people in the U.S.[113]

The weak connection between charitable donations and anti-poverty activities has been a source of considerable controversy in the philanthropic community. One possibility is that donors like to give money to the community where they live, yet wealthy people do not tend to live in communities where there are numerous poor people. Wealthy donors give primarily for education and health, areas where programs do not tend to have an anti-poverty focus. Another possibility is that donors do not fully understand where their dollars go. For example, for donors with incomes below $100,000 per year, religious giving comprises two-thirds of donations. Donors may not be aware that less than 20 cents of every dollar given to religious organizations funds programs for the economically disadvantaged. Or maybe donors know what they are doing and they prefer to give to broad-based causes that help everyone, including the poor.[114]

In an era when revenues to government are in short supply to support basic public functions (including the governmental safety net), questions are being raised about whether IRS treatment of charity should be so generous. U.S. law not only confers upon nonprofit 501(c)(3) organizations the privilege of not paying taxes on income, it also grants tax deductions to those who make donations to these organizations. Compared to countries around the world, the U.S. tax system has been described as the most generous to philanthropy.[115] One analyst has noted that the foregone revenue from the charitable deduction alone is greater than the total amount that the federal government spends each year on cash assistance for the nondisabled poor.[116] The question becomes, then, whether the poor would be better off if the government had more revenues for the safety net, even if it meant less charitable giving.

Types of Giving for Anti-Poverty Activities

Among philanthropists dedicated to reducing poverty in America, a schism has developed between advocates of two general types of donations: those that directly help meet the basic needs of low-income families versus those that support advocacy for the poor or support innovative policy experiments aimed at poverty reduction. The latter form of donation is sometimes called "impact philanthropy," in contrast to donations aimed at direct assistance for people in need. Through impact philanthropy, the donor seeks to maximize the effect of their gift by helping, indirectly, multiple communities of low-income people. Unfortunately, there is no national database that defines the relative magnitude or trends in the two types of philanthropy.

The Michigan Recession and Recovery Study (October 2009–April 2010) provides an excellent illustration of the value of charitable donations that go directly to help families in need. At the time of this study, roughly one in seven households (15 percent) in the Detroit Metropolitan area were in poverty and another 14.3 percent were living with incomes between 100 percent and 200 percent of the poverty line (the near poor). The study examined how low-income households were making ends meet in this vulnerable period immediately after the official end of the Great Recession.

The authors found that 78.8 percent of the poor and near-poor (including 90 percent of blacks and 67 percent of whites) received cash or in-kind benefits from at least one government program. Those unemployed more than six months were more likely to receive benefits from multiple government programs than those with shorter bouts of unemployment. Unemployment Insurance was shown to be particularly important.

The long-term unemployed, however, were also the most likely to have received private support. In the previous year, 75.4 percent received private support from family, friends, and non-profit charities. And 59.7 percent of the long-term unemployed combined governmental and private support. The authors concluded that charity of various forms was an important source of support for basic needs among the long-term unemployed in the Detroit metropolitan area.[117]

Instead of giving directly to the poor, some prefer system-wide approaches to giving that will help many more impoverished people. The tension between the two camps of anti-poverty philanthropists was illustrated in October 2011 when several dozen homeless people slept outside the impressive $500 million headquarters of the Bill and Melinda Gates Foundation in Seattle.

The homeless were protesting a $30-million cut in government support that had caused some shelters in Seattle to be closed. They were seeking a $30,000 award from the Gates Foundation to reopen the shelters. The $30,000 request to a Foundation with $37 billion in assets drew significant media attention. The government ultimately reinstated the cuts and the publicity was not always fair to the Gates Foundation (which had already spent $47 million on transitional housing and homeless assistance for families in the Pacific Northwest). But a spokesperson for the Gates Foundation also made this pointed remark: "We're trying to move upstream to a systems level to either prevent homelessness before it happens or to end it as soon as possible after it happens."[118] This is another way of saying that the Gates Foundation is interested in a stronger focus on impact philanthropy.

Anti-poverty advocates, who often do their work in Washington, DC, or state capitals, are classic recipients of impact philanthropy. They include a wide range of non-profit organizations, from the Southern Poverty Law Center (Jackson, Mississippi) to the Center for Budget and Policy Priorities (Washington, DC). Through White Papers, testimony, media outreach, and other activities, these groups try to influence the course of community thinking and public policy in ways that will help low-income families. Since such organizations need to be free to criticize government policies, they are very reluctant to accept government funding. As a result, charitable donations are critical to their sustainability.[119]

In recent years, there has been increasing interest in a new type of anti-poverty effort that combines direct assistance of people in need with an experimental or public policy component. Perhaps the flagship version of this hybrid intervention was launched by philanthropist and New York City Mayor Michael Bloomberg in 2006.[120] Bloomberg's Center for Economic Opportunity was authorized to use tax credits and financial incentives to motivate low-income adults to address the five factors that research shows give rise to poverty: lack of early childhood care, poor education of at-risk young adults, lack of jobs for disadvantaged young adults, insufficient assets and savings among the working poor, and lack of job skills among the working poor. In 2012, the Center won Harvard's Innovations in Government Award for its anti-poverty programs,[121] despite the claims of some critics that the Center had not made a detectable dent in New York City's poverty problem.[122] The Center also won a federal grant to replicate successful measures in other cities around the United States.

Although the Center has launched more than 50 initiatives since its inception,[123] the flagship experiment implemented "conditional cash transfers" (CCTs) with entirely philanthropic dollars. The CCT is a form of welfare payment that is conditioned on good behavior by the recipient, a concept that was used successfully in Mexico prior to the experiment in New York City. Launched in September 2007 and called "Opportunity NYC—Family Rewards," the CCT program went beyond encouraging recipients to work by including rewards for good decisions about education and health. Cash awards were made for 22 specific behaviors.

In a remarkably rigorous design, CCTs were evaluated in a randomized trial involving approximately 4,800 families and 11,000 children in six impoverished areas of New York City. Half of the participants received CCTs averaging $6,000, and half were assigned to a control group that did not receive cash incentives. Parents were given payments for actions like going to the dentist ($100) or holding down a full-time job ($150 per month). Children were rewarded for regular school attendance ($25–$50 per month) or passing a high school Regents exam ($600).

A formal evaluation of the trial released in 2010 (after two years of the three-year experiment) showed mixed results, for example, school-related outcomes did not improve for elementary and middle school students, but high school students in the CCT program had better attendance, higher rates of grade advancement, and better test scores than their counterparts not in the program.[124] Based on the experience, New York City decided to terminate the program rather than move into a phase that would require financing with public money.[125] Nonetheless, what is distinctive about this philanthropic program is a combination of direct assistance to people in need with an agenda of public policy change based on scientific evaluation of an experiment.

Anti-Poverty Giving and the Great Recession

In order to assess the impact of the Great Recession and the slow recovery on donations with an anti-poverty impact, it would be ideal to have a yearly time series of donations that are known to impact poverty in America. Unfortunately and disturbingly, there are no systematic data on how many donations are aimed at reducing poverty each year and the effect of such donations.

What we do know is that the potential donors, those with substantial income and wealth, took a very big hit in the Great Recession.[126] In 2007 and 2009, the federal government interviewed and re-interviewed a large sample of American families about their finances. Median household income declined only modestly (from $50,100 to $49,800), but those in the top quartile of the wealth distribution experienced a 13 percent drop in household income. Median household wealth took a bigger dive, from $125,000 to $96,000. Mean household wealth, which is strongly influenced by high-wealth households, dropped more sharply, from $595,000 to $481,000.[127] These data are significant, since they indicate that the pocketbooks of the potential givers in America, especially the big givers, were squeezed by the Great Recession.

In order to examine what happened in the first full year after the Great Recession (2010), a slightly different comparison must be made. The family finances of a random sample of U.S. households in 2007 can be compared to the finances of a random sample of U.S. households in 2010. Median family income declined from $49,600 in 2007 to $45,800 in 2010. Mean household wealth was down in all quintiles of the wealth distribution except the bottom quintile. In the top ten percent of the wealth distribution, mean household wealth declined from $3.475 million in 2007 to $2.944 million in 2010. The median household was left with no more wealth in 2010 than it had in the early 1990s, and the drop from 2007 to 2010 was from $126,400 to $77,300.[128]

In an analysis about poverty, it may seem strange to be looking at the finances of the wealthiest Americans. In this chapter, however, our focus is on charitable donations and it is well known that the giving behavior of wealthy Americans has a powerful impact on overall giving. In light of these trends (which were certainly driven to a significant extent by the collapse of the stock market and the collapse of housing prices), we should begin with an expectation that the annual growth rate of philanthropic donations may have been adversely affected by the Great Recession.

The data confirm this hypothesis. Charitable donations rose steadily until reaching their peak in 2007. They dropped significantly in 2008 and 2009 and then began a slow recovery in 2010 and 2011. The total amount of charitable giving in 2011, $298.4 billion, was still $11 billion below the 2007 peak. Since 1971, the average inflation-adjusted rate of growth in total charitable donations in the United States slowed for the two years after each recession. The two years after the Great Recession (2010–11) saw the second-slowest growth rate of any two-year period since 1971, the exception being the two years following the 2001 recession, which was exacerbated by the events of 9/11.

While overall charitable giving was hurt by the Great Recession, perhaps the will to give for the poor held up better, presumably because the hardships of low-income families are more salient in a severe recession. Unfortunately, there is no consistently collected data on charitable donations for anti-poverty efforts in the United States.

As a surrogate for anti-poverty efforts, let us consider the category in *Giving USA* called "human services." As explained by the IU Center on Philanthropy, this category includes charities focused on courts and legal services, employment and vocational training, food and nutrition, long-term housing and temporary shelter, public safety and community disaster relief, recreation and sports, youth development, family and children's services, emergency assistance for families, and self-sufficiency for women, seniors, veterans, and individuals with disabilities.

The human services category is certainly an imperfect surrogate for charity aimed at reducing poverty in America. Some of the recipients live outside of the United States. Some recipients are poor, but some are probably near poor or lower-middle class. And some of the activities (e.g., sports and recreation) could include programs that are not aimed at meeting the basic needs of families. Nonetheless, it is probably the best surrogate that is publicly available for use by scholars.

The annual data from *Giving USA* show that inflation-adjusted giving for human services rose steadily from 2003 to 2007, reaching a peak of $31 billion in 2007. It then dropped sharply (-15.9 percent) in 2008, recovered slightly in 2009 but then declined slightly in both 2010 and 2011. In short, giving for human services took a big hit in the Great Recession and was slow to recover.

In summary, Queen Elizabeth made a controversial decision in sixteenth-century England that private philanthropy was not adequate to meet the needs of the deserving poor. She established a national policy of anti-poverty responsibilities that were to be implemented by government at the local level. The United States has followed the path of Elizabethan England. When faced with the reality of the Great Recession of 2007–09, Presidents George W. Bush and Barack Obama and the U.S. Congress knew that they could not rely entirely on charity to help families in need. In the next chapter, we shall explore how the governmental safety net responded to the Great Recession.

4
America's Partial Safety Net

Over the last 75 years, the United States has built a safety net to offer protection for low-income[129] individuals and families as well as other individuals who become unemployed. The phrase "low-income" refers generally to people who are poor or near-poor, usually with incomes less than some multiple of the official poverty line (e.g., 185% or 300%). Comprised of governmental assistance programs and tax provisions, the net is a complex combination of state and federal policies. Many of the various public programs have their roots in—or were expanded due to—President Lyndon Johnson's "War on Poverty." In his 1964 State of the Union Address, Johnson said, "This administration today, here and now, declares unconditional war on poverty in America. I urge this Congress and all Americans to join with me in that effort . . . we shall not rest until that war is won. The richest nation on earth can afford to win it. We cannot afford to lose it." Yet, Johnson's vision was not fully realized, and thus we term the safety net to be "partial" because it does not eradicate poverty in this country. As we shall see, parts of it are less responsive than others to economic downturns.

Before turning to the individual programs and their performance during the recession, several issues should be addressed. Although the phrase "safety net" appears to be simple, it represents a wide range of different programs and services that operate at multiple levels of government and in both the private and public sectors. Unfortunately, there is no single data source in the United States that regularly supplies basic data on America's safety net: how many low-income people are assisted by year, the degree of assistance, the consequences of the assistance, who paid for the assistance, and the overall cost of the safety net (and its components).

Second, in Western European nations, the safety net is often organized in conjunction with social insurance systems that benefit the elderly or other non-working adults. In the United States, however, social insurance programs (such as Medicare and Social Security) are often seen as different from anti-poverty programs because a worker, who may be defined as middle class, pays taxes on a regular basis with a perception that those tax revenues are accumulated in national trust funds. The assumption is that those funds will ultimately be used to provide benefits to the worker when he or she becomes old enough (or otherwise eligible) for social insurance benefits (e.g., Medicare and Social Security). Although such perceptions may be oversimplified, they cause people in the United States—and their politicians—to treat Medicare and Social Security differently than the safety-net programs aimed at meeting the needs of people who are temporarily or chronically poor.

The beneficiaries of the safety net may draw resources temporarily (e.g., due to an unanticipated spell of unemployment or reduced hours of work) or they may do so permanently (e.g., due to a disability that precludes work or chronic inability to find work). In the design of the safety net, a key question is how to ensure that able-bodied recipients have appropriate incentives to find work and function without assistance from the safety net. Thus, some anti-poverty programs have work requirements and/or provisions designed to encourage recipients to work.

The forms of assistance offered through the safety net vary. Cash assistance provides the recipient families the largest degree of flexibility, but there is no assurance that the heads of household will expend the cash on the most essential household needs. In-kind assistance may only be used for specified purposes as illustrated by food assistance programs, subsidized health care, and vouchers for housing payments.

All but two of the public programs considered in this chapter are means-tested. That is, in order to be eligible, individuals/families must meet certain financial requirements, namely having very low income and assets. The cash or in-kind benefits provided by these programs are intended to buffer vulnerable individuals and families from experiencing hardship (or further hardship) because of their very low income. By contrast, receipt of Unemployment Insurance (UI) benefits is based upon job loss, not low income. However, its purpose, like means-tested programs, is to support individuals during a vulnerable time. The Earned Income Tax Credit (EITC), which provides a refundable credit to low- and moderate-income workers, is means-tested in the sense that workers with wages above a certain threshold will not receive it. But unlike other means-tested programs, the EITC is designed to supplement earnings, not necessarily provide a "net" for those who are experiencing difficult times. Over the last 15 years, the EITC has become a significant source of support for low-income families.[130]

Another distinction between these various programs is their funding structure. *Entitlement* programs mandate spending for eligible people according to criteria established in law; *discretionary* programs assist low-income people to the extent that yearly appropriations permit. A discretionary program is sometimes implemented as a "block grant" from the federal government to the states, which means that states have wide discretion in how the funds are expended. The programs vary in terms of who picks up the tab: the federal government, the state government, or a combination of the two.

Although the literature on the safety net is large and complex, two findings are well established. First, the net has been far more effective at reducing poverty among the elderly than it has been in reducing poverty among working-age adults and children. Second, some safety net programs may create some work disincentives, but these behavioral effects are generally small compared to the direct poverty-reducing impact of the government assistance.[131]

In this chapter, we examine how several key programs in the safety net responded to the Great Recession and its aftermath. The focus is on programs that provide food, medical care, housing, and cash assistance to low-income and unemployed Americans. In addition to direct assistance programs, we also consider the Earned Income Tax Credit (EITC), which is now considered part of the safety net. Our coverage of the safety net is not comprehensive. For example, we do not examine the federal block grant to the states for child care assistance, which is designed to help with child care payments for children with special needs and children in families with very low income. Other excluded programs include Head Start; Women, Infants, and Children (WIC); Child Support Enforcement; and federal low-income energy assistance. In the next chapter, we note that some of these smaller programs are vulnerable to cutbacks due to fiscal pressures on state and local governments.

Supplemental Nutrition Assistance Program (SNAP)

Formerly called "Food Stamps," SNAP is a federal program that enables low-income persons to buy food through use of Electronic Benefits Transfer (EBT) cards. It is the largest federal food and nutrition program. These cards function like a debit card, but holders may only purchase basic foods (i.e., items such as personal products, alcohol/tobacco, pre-prepared hot food, and cleaning supplies are excluded).

SNAP is overseen by the U.S. Department of Agriculture (USDA), and it is administered by offices in each of the 50 states under USDA rules and oversight. USDA pays for 100 percent of the benefits, but shares the administrative costs on a 50–50 basis with the states. SNAP is an entitlement, meaning that anyone who meets the eligibility requirements and applies for assistance receives a benefit, regardless of the near term fiscal condition of federal and state governments. The program is therefore quite responsive to economic conditions, and SNAP caseloads tend to rise in recessions and fall during periods of economic prosperity.

For the first time in history, the monthly number of people using SNAP benefits in 2010 exceeded the 40 million mark (see Figure 4).[132] Today, roughly one in every eight Americans benefits from SNAP. The average monthly SNAP benefit in fiscal year 2012 is projected to be $133.84 per person and $283.96 per household.[133] In fiscal year 2012 alone, approximately $73.5 billion will be spent on SNAP by the U.S. Department of Agriculture.[134]

Figure 4. Change in Average Annual SNAP Caseloads: 2006-2011.*

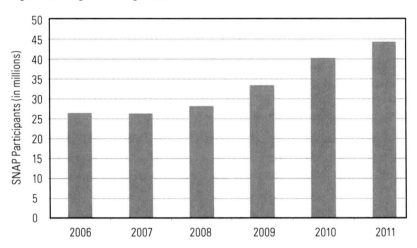

*2011 data are calculated through June.
Source: USDA: http://www.fns.usda.gov/pd/SNAPsummary.htm.

Federal spending on SNAP is determined by three factors: the number of eligible individuals, the share of the eligibles who enroll (the "take-up rate" or "participation rate"), and the benefit level that is received. Each of the three variables is influenced by economic conditions.

Eligibility for SNAP assistance is determined primarily by income, but assets and resources also play a role. From 2006 to 2009 (the latest year for which eligibility estimates are available), the number of individuals eligible for SNAP assistance increased by 22 percent, from 36.5 million to 44.5 million.[135] Although much of this growth appears to be linked to economic conditions, there was also some easing of eligibility requirements that contributed to the boost in the number of eligibles. During this same period (2006 to 2009), SNAP caseloads increased at an even faster clip than the number of eligibles, suggesting that the SNAP take-up rate is on the rise. Take-up rates are believed to be increasing for several reasons: eligible families are experiencing greater financial hardship due to the Great Recession and lingering unemployment problems, USDA and state offices are engaging in more effective outreach, and the stigma associated with program participation may be less when more people are participating.[136]

States differ significantly in their estimated SNAP participation rates, from an estimated high of 94 percent in Maine in 2008 to a low of 46 percent in Wyoming.[137] The Midwest has a significantly higher participation rate, at 74 percent, while the Southwest and West have significantly lower participation rates, at 61 percent and 58 percent, respectively. The reasons behind these state and regional differences are not fully understood.

The average monthly benefit under SNAP has also increased. From 2007 to 2010, the average monthly benefit increased by almost 40 percent, from $96 to $134. This pattern is not surprising since income levels of the eligible population are likely depressed by the forces of the Great Recession, making them eligible to receive larger SNAP benefits.

With the declining federal commitment to cash welfare assistance (see discussion of TANF below) since 1996, SNAP has become an extremely important source of assistance for working mothers and their children, especially the working poor and near poor. An estimated 40 percent of single mothers with incomes between 100 to 130 percent of the poverty line received SNAP benefits.[138] Overall, the number of low-income working households on SNAP has nearly tripled in the last decade.[139]

In response to the Great Recession, SNAP spending was increased in the 2009 federal stimulus package. The large, temporary boost in SNAP spending (roughly $20 billion over 18 months) was triggered by several changes in program design and administration. The average SNAP benefit was boosted 15 percent. The three-month time limit on benefits for able-bodied adults without children was eliminated temporarily. Income eligibility requirements were eased somewhat. And the liquid asset limits in most states were changed from $2,000–$3,000 to a suggested national uniform figure of $10,000.[140] With regard to administration, states were given more discretion to skip a face-to-face interview when determining initial eligibility and when recertifying eligibility. States were also encouraged to automatically make TANF recipients eligible for SNAP assistance.[141]

Although a more generous SNAP program seems appropriate in the aftermath of the Great Recession, the higher rate of SNAP spending may exacerbate fiscal concerns in some corners and could trigger opposition among some taxpayers. The enlarged SNAP benefit level was originally scheduled to last until 2018 but expiration was later moved up to November 2013 (at an estimated fiscal savings of $14 billion over ten years).[142] Looking to the future, there are three indications that SNAP, even though it is arguably one of the most effective of America's safety-net programs,[143] could be at risk of stricter budgetary controls.

First, since spending on entitlement programs is more difficult for politicians to control than spending on block grants, some politicians have suggested converting SNAP into a block grant to the states.[144] The idea is to make SNAP more like Temporary Assistance for Needy Families (TANF—described further below), thereby giving more flexibility to the states to adjust eligibility, outreach, and benefit levels. However, TANF, a federal cash assistance program, has worked less effectively than SNAP during economic downturns.[145] Although there are no proposals currently before Congress to convert SNAP into a block grant in the near-term, the idea may gain greater support in Congress if the federal budget is not placed on a sustainable fiscal path. In June 2012, the Senate Farm Bill, though not yet passed nor signed into law at the time of this writing, contained substantial cuts to SNAP funding.[146] The House version of the Farm Bill (the Lucas-Peterson bill) would make even deeper cuts, primarily by eliminating "categorically eligible recipients"—individuals and families who are automatically eligible for SNAP because they receive (or are eligible to receive) other government benefits, including noncash benefits under TANF. An analysis of USDA data by the Center on Budget and Policy Priorities finds that the typical family who would lose benefits under the Lucas-Peterson proposal is headed by a working single mother whose gross income puts her just over traditional SNAP eligibility limits but who has rent and child care costs that are half or more of her take-home pay.[147]

Second, media reports have brought to light that a few wealthy individuals are receiving SNAP.[148] Despite the isolated nature of these reported incidents, if public confidence in SNAP deteriorates further, more stringent reforms of SNAP may be appealing to politicians.[149]

Finally, the uncertain work requirements in the SNAP program are triggering scrutiny. In theory, the work requirements covering SNAP recipients are strong, at least for the 40 percent of recipients who are non-disabled, non-elderly adults. These SNAP recipients must register for work, search for work, and accept a job if offered. A SNAP recipient may not quit a job or voluntarily reduce work to less than 30 hours per week. Able-bodied adults without dependents (ABAWDs) must work at least 20 hours per week or they can qualify for only three months of SNAP benefits in a 36-month period. However, the ABAWD requirements under SNAP were suspended in 2009 and 2010 due to the poor state of the economy, and the Obama administration sought another extension for 2013 due to the slow economic recovery. Enforcement of the SNAP work requirement is left to the states but states do not have to meet a minimum work participation rate like they do under TANF. Sanctions for failure to enforce SNAP work requirements are rarely imposed on states or individuals. Some poverty scholars are advocating stronger enforcement of work requirements under SNAP, in part because they believe fiscal savings will result in the long run.[150] On the other hand, in 2010 the majority of SNAP households with a non-disabled, working aged adult were working, calling into question the need for stronger enforcement of work requirements.[151]

Medicaid and Child Health Insurance Program (CHIP)

Medicaid is a health insurance program for eligible low-income individuals. The program is administered jointly by the U.S. Department of Health and Human Services (HHS) and the 50 states. Funding for Medicaid comes from a complex formula that entails matching of dollars provided by federal and state governments. States with lower per capita incomes are eligible for a larger Medicaid match from HHS.

The Medicaid program provides coverage for a basic set of services ("mandatory benefits") such as physician visits and hospital stays. States also have the option of providing additional coverage for services such as dental visits and physical therapy. The more generous the state program, the higher the costs are to both the state and the federal government.

Eligibility for Medicaid varies by state, but family income, resources, and assets are important criteria and certain groups of people (e.g., the blind and disabled) are automatically eligible. All states must cover all pregnant women and young children in families with incomes less than 133 percent of the official poverty line. Children ages 6 to 19 must be covered if they are in families with incomes below the official poverty line. Eligibility criteria for adults are left primarily to the states. Medicaid is a separate program from Medicare, the public health insurance program that is available to those 65 years of age or older and certain younger adults with disabilities.

Unlike SNAP, Medicaid does not provide purchasing power directly to the eligible beneficiary. Instead, the program is designed to send payments to health care providers who agree to care for Medicaid-eligible individuals. Many states also require the Medicaid beneficiary to pay small amounts of cost sharing (e.g., a co-payment for certain services).

CHIP, enacted in 1997, is a joint program of the federal government and the states that provides health insurance coverage for children under the age of 19 whose parents or guardians are not eligible for Medicaid. It is administered as a block grant. Federal funds may be used for children (and in some cases adults) from targeted households with incomes above the poverty line. States can implement CHIP as an expansion of Medicaid coverage and/or they can establish a separate program for CHIP-eligible children.[152]

Like SNAP, Medicaid is an entitlement program. All eligible individuals who enroll receive coverage, regardless of the near-term fiscal condition of the federal government or the states. CHIP is capped by the funds available to a state each year. Thus, Medicaid enrollments—more so than CHIP enrollments—tend to rise during recessions and decline when the economy is prosperous.

Medicaid enrollment has grown by 7.6 million, or by 17.8 percent, since the Great Recession began in December 2007. In June 2010 a record enrollment of 50.3 million was reached as many Americans lost their jobs and, with those jobs, their employer-provided health insurance.[153]

In 2010 Congress passed a comprehensive health-care reform bill (the "Affordable Care Act"), but many of the Act's key provisions do not take effect until 2014 or later. After the Supreme Court upheld the constitutionality of the Affordable Care Act in 2012, states began to work intensively for implementation of the Act, including a large expansion in the Medicaid program.

When the Affordable Care Act was enacted in March 2010, Congress anticipated that states might be tempted to reduce their Medicaid spending by curtailing eligibility or reducing enrollment through changes in enrollment procedures. Under the Affordable Care Act, states are prohibited from curbing eligibility and enrollments through 2014. At that time, Congress calls for a substantial expansion of Medicaid to cover everyone—including adults—with incomes under 133 percent of the official federal poverty line. States are provided new federal funding to help cover most of this program expansion. As a result, nearly all states "held steady" or made targeted expansions in their eligibility and enrollment rules in 2010, with a total of 13 states expanding eligibility and 14 states accelerating enrollment and renewal procedures. However, as of this writing, a small number of states, including the populous state of Texas, have indicated that they will decline the new federal money and not expand their Medicaid programs.

In order to help states adjust to the rapid growth of Medicaid enrollments, the 2009 stimulus package provided $103 billion in federal fiscal relief to the states. The relief was designed as a temporary boost in the federal matching rates for the costs incurred by state Medicaid programs. The relief took effect on October 1, 2008 and expired on June 30, 2011.

In the midst of the Great Recession, Congress took special pains to ensure that more low-income children were covered for basic health care. In January 2009, Congress enacted a substantial expansion of the CHIP program that is projected to increase the number of enrolled children from 7 to 11 million. A key change in eligibility allows federal funds to be used for families with incomes up to 300 percent of the poverty line, a limit that was boosted up from 200 percent. The expansion was financed by higher taxes on cigarettes and other tobacco products.[154]

While Medicaid did respond robustly to the Great Recession, in part due to Congressional action, the future of the Medicaid program is somewhat uncertain. In the near term, many states are responding to the expiration of federal stimulus funds by reducing payment rates to doctors and hospitals, eliminating optional benefits, and increasing the co-payments that beneficiaries must pay.

When Congress passed the Affordable Care Act in 2010, it did so without a single Republican vote. With more Republicans in Congress after the November 2010 elections, there were calls for repeal of the health care reform law, even before it could be implemented and evaluated. In January 2011, for instance, the House of Representatives voted 245–189 to repeal the law, but the Senate rejected the repeal effort a few weeks later on a 51–47 vote.[155] Given this impasse, it is expected that health care will be a major issue in the 2012 presidential and congressional elections. However, it seems unlikely that the Affordable Care Act will be repealed, although certain provisions of the law could be delayed or repealed by the Congress.

For low-income populations, Medicaid and CHIP were the key medical features of the safety net during the Great Recession, and they played a critical role during the recovery. Starting in 2014, the Affordable Care Act will expand Medicaid coverage to many of the poor, new poor, and near poor who are not currently covered. However, the Medicaid program is so expensive, to states as well as the federal government, that it is a target for fiscal restraint by budget officials and policy makers.

Temporary Assistance to Needy Families (TANF)

Enacted as part of the 1996 welfare-reform act, TANF replaced the federal entitlement program called Aid to Families with Dependent Children (AFDC). TANF provides cash and other forms of assistance to needy families with dependent children. Due to stringent eligibility rules for two-parent families, it is a program that primarily serves single-parent (usually single-mother) households. The program is administered by the U.S. Department of Health and Human Services (HHS) as a block grant to the states.

TANF funds may be expended for any of these four general purposes: (1) to help families care for children in their own homes or in the homes of relatives, (2) to reduce dependence on government through job training, work, and marriage, (3) to reduce out-of-wedlock pregnancies, and (4) to encourage the formation of two-parent families. The types of assistance generally provided are cash benefits, child care, transportation, education, and job training, with cash benefits being the largest category.

TANF's predecessor, AFDC, was an entitlement program that provided cash assistance to very poor families with minor children. Due to concerns that AFDC provided a disincentive to work, Congress overhauled the program, placing a lifetime limit of 60 months on federal TANF assistance. Some states have adopted even shorter time limits. TANF also requires that recipients be working or participating in work preparation activities. For example, at least half of a state's TANF caseload must work at least 30 hours a week (or a lesser amount if they are single parents with young children) or face possible financial penalties from the federal government. Whether due to these reforms, a strong economy in the late 1990s when TANF was implemented, or other policy changes such as the EITC expansions (discussed below), the number of households receiving TANF fell by more than half. Six years after its enactment, TANF served less than half of all eligible families, as opposed to AFDC, which typically served between 80 and 85 percent of all eligibles.[156]

The federal TANF funding provided to the states is not cost-free. States must also spend some of their own dollars to comply with the "maintenance of effort" (MOE) requirement. Those state funds supplement the $16.6 billion yearly federal block grant, which has been unchanged since 1997. In fiscal year 2009, for example, expenditures under TANF and the MOE requirement totaled approximately $33.5 billion.[157]

How much cash a family receives each month from TANF is dependent upon family size, other income, and other factors. There is also substantial variation in the generosity of TANF cash benefit levels across the 50 states. The maximum monthly TANF benefit (the amount a family of a certain size would receive if they had no other income) is generally low in the Southern states (less than

$300 a month for a family of three), while Alaska, California, Hawaii, New Hampshire, and Wisconsin are the most generous states (benefit levels $500 or more per month). Benefit levels that are less than $300 per month for a family of three annualize to less than 20 percent of the poverty threshold. Benefits fall below 30 percent of the poverty line in the majority of states. Further, when adjusted for inflation, a majority of states have actually reduced their TANF benefit levels from 2006 to 2010.[158] While most TANF families are also eligible for SNAP, Medicaid, and some other state and federal programs, TANF is the major source of cash assistance available.

Unlike SNAP and Medicaid, which are safety net programs that have responded robustly to the Great Recession, TANF assistance has not been highly responsive to recent financial hardships. Average monthly TANF caseloads declined slightly from 2006 to 2008 and then rose from 2009 to 2011 (although not in all states). However, that increase does not account for the many more families that are likely eligible for TANF and are not using it. From December 2007 to December 2009, the heart of the Great Recession, SNAP caseloads increased by almost 50 percent while TANF case loads grew by just 13 percent. Although some of the recent increase in number of individuals receiving SNAP are due to changes in eligibility and outreach activities that inform the public about SNAP, it is generally accepted that SNAP, as an entitlement program, responds to economic downturns more thoroughly than TANF and other block grant programs that rely on yearly budget decisions by elected officials or otherwise have fixed budgets.[159] The work requirements embedded within TANF give states an incentive to serve relatively few households. In order to meet a 50 percent work participation rate and not suffer potential financial penalties, states may put into place conditions, such as stringent upfront job search requirements, that make it easier to identify individuals who are more likely to find jobs (and thus contribute to the work participation rate) and deny benefits to those who have difficulties securing work.[160]

Given both the difficulties in obtaining TANF benefits and the slowing economy, it is not surprising that the ranks are growing of poor single-parent families who appear to be without any form of cash assistance or income from work. Called the "disconnected," because they are disconnected from the labor force and from cash assistance, an estimated 1.2 million poor women and their children were disconnected for at least four consecutive months in 2008, and preliminary work with newer data indicates an increase.[161] The disconnected seem to be a group who has slipped through holes in the safety net.

As part of the Recovery Act of 2009, TANF "Emergency Funds" were authorized. States that had experienced caseload growth or increases in the cost of basic services could apply for these funds, which could be used to provide basic cash assistance, short-term, non-recurring benefits (for example, a one-time payment to help with rent), or to fund subsidized employment programs.[162] The latter offer subsidies to employers to hire unemployed TANF recipients. All states except Wyoming received TANF Emergency Funds, and 37 states ran subsidized jobs programs, employing 250,000 adults and youth.[163] However, the funds expired at the end of 2009 and were not renewed by Congress.

Overall, one of the central problems with TANF is that the $16.5-billion block grant to the states has been left unchanged by Congress since TANF was created in the mid-1990s. Due to the gradual effects of inflation, the purchasing power of the TANF block grant has already been eroded by about 33 percent.[164] Moreover, federal TANF funding is not sensitive to the business cycle and thus, when the rate of long-term unemployment rises sharply, as it did during and after the Great Recession, states were left to their own devices to respond to the burgeoning number of families in need of cash assistance—except for the Emergency Funds authorized by Congress. And states were held to the same work participation rates, despite high unemployment. For some children in poverty, a different federal program began to fill some of the void created by the declining rate of inflation-adjusted federal spending on TANF.

Supplemental Security Income (SSI)

Supplemental Security Income (SSI) is the other major federal cash assistance program available to low-income (and low asset) individuals, but only if they are blind, aged, or disabled. SSI is an entitlement program, funded out of federal general funds and overseen by the Social Security Administration (SSA). The income limits are based on poverty determinations while the asset limits on eligibility in 2010 were $2,000 for individuals and $3,000 for couples, though some exceptions to these limits are permitted.

Monthly SSI benefit levels are set nationally to be uniform across states and are generally much higher than TANF benefits. In 2010–11, the basic SSI monthly benefit was $674 per person, and $1,011 per couple. Since the benefit declines as other sources of income rise, the average monthly benefit in November 2010 was $499.[165] By May 2012 it had risen to $516 per month. There are no time limits or work requirements associated with receipt of benefits, and some states provide a supplement to the federal SSI benefit.[166]

Although SSI was launched in 1972 in the aftermath of LBJ's War on Poverty, it was modified by Congress in the 1996 welfare reform act. It made legal non-citizens (e.g., immigrants) ineligible for benefits (although some were subsequently reinstated), imposed stricter criteria for determining disability in children, and eliminated drug and/or alcohol dependence as a diagnosis that could qualify an adult for benefits. Unlike TANF, these changes did not reduce the number of recipients, they merely slowed growth.[167]

The type of individual who receives SSI has shifted over time. Low-income elderly recipients were the primary beneficiaries when the program started in the 1970s, but disabled adults now comprise the largest share of recipients.[168] About 85 percent of all SSI recipients are eligible due to a disability determination (as opposed to old age) and six in ten of the disabled recipients are mentally disabled.

In May 2012, there were 8.2 million SSI recipients, including about 2.8 million who receive both SSI and Social Security.[169] In most states, SSI benefits automatically trigger Medicaid eligibility. About half of SSI recipients also receive SNAP; about 20 percent receive federal housing assistance.

One of the fastest-growing components of SSI has been the program for disabled children, which served 1.3 million children in 2011. A disabled child is eligible for the same basic benefit ($674 per month) as a disabled adult. The child's disability must be "marked and severe" and the child's family must meet the SSI income and asset requirements. The child may stay on SSI as long as they are a minor and are disabled. In contrast, TANF has a five-year limit.

One of the rationales for the child benefit is that a disabled child may impair the earnings potential of parents and impose extra costs on those parents. According to one estimate, the annual size of the child benefit is within $1,000 of the sum of the direct costs and average earnings losses induced by care for a disabled child.[170] Recent research suggests that SSI support reduces the rate of childhood poverty without reducing the family's earnings or incentive to work.[171]

The number of SSI recipients hovered around 4 million from 1974 to 1982 and then rose steadily to 6.5 million in 1993. There was only slight growth until 2000, but by 2006 the number of recipients had passed the 7 million mark. From 2006 to mid-2012 the number of SSI recipients increased from 7 million to about 8.2 million.[172]

As a disability program, one might not expect use of SSI to be affected by the Great Recession. While there is no definitive research on this issue, there are several reasons to believe SSI has grown due to the Great Recession. First, states share the cost of administering and funding TANF, whose federal contributions are fixed. The federal government funds SSI entirely, so during tough budgetary times, states may have an incentive to encourage eligible families to pursue SSI rather than TANF.[173] Second, individuals, particularly older adults, who were laid off or lost jobs might turn to SSI if they do not qualify for—or if they lose—Unemployment Insurance benefits (see below).[174] Of course, these individuals would still need to qualify for benefits, but many disabled people are employed and could potentially receive SSI if they lost their jobs. Finally, recent evidence shows that workers with disabilities were disproportionately affected by the recession, with the proportion of workers with a disability declining 9 percent over the 2007–09 period.[175] Thus, these otherwise eligible individuals may turn to SSI as a means for supporting themselves.

As federal budgetary pressures mount, the SSI program for children may be targeted for scrutiny. SSI lists about 100 mental and physical impairments that allow a child to qualify, although a 1994 U.S. Supreme Court decision compelled SSI to add a functional limitation test that is typically based on evidence supplied by parents, teachers, and other sources. The 47 percent rate of child enrollment growth in SSI from 2000 to 2010 is primarily concentrated in categories where the disability determination has a degree of subjectivity (e.g., speech and language disabilities and attention-deficit/hyperactivity disorders). However, the rate of approval for applications into the programs has been stable at around 40 percent. Some policy analysts have suggested periodic disability reviews for children who receive SSI benefits, since each $1 spent on such reviews may save $12.5 in spending.[176]

Housing Assistance

The federal government provides housing assistance to low-income Americans through three primary programs: traditional public housing projects, a demand-side housing voucher program that allows eligible families to choose a unit in the private market and pay less than the market rent, and a supply-side subsidy program that encourages owners and developers to offer housing at below-market rates so that low-income families can afford them. In 2010, nearly 5 million low-income families received federal housing support, 1.2 million through public housing, 2.1 million through tenant-oriented assistance and 1.1 million through subsidies to developers.[177] All three programs are administered through 2,600 state, regional, and local housing agencies under the oversight of the U.S. Department of Housing and Urban Development (HUD).[178]

Like TANF, the HUD housing assistance programs are not entitlement programs. Eligibility determinations for public housing and housing vouchers are based on income and family size, and HUD expects that state and local agencies will expend at least 75 percent of the funds on families whose incomes do not exceed 30 percent of median income in the area. Family incomes of beneficiaries may not exceed 50 percent of median income. Since HUD's budgetary outlays are small relative to the size of the eligible population, it is common for eligible families to wait many months or even years before they are selected from an agency's waiting list. Those selections are often made by lottery, but in some states other selection procedures are also used.

The maximum subsidy for public housing that HUD pays is typically equal to a specified "fair market rent" minus 30 percent of gross family income. Specifically, the rent paid by a public housing tenant is the highest of the following: (1) 30 percent of the monthly adjusted income less deductions allowed by the regulations; (2) 10 percent of monthly income; (3) welfare rent, if applicable; or (4) a $25 minimum rent or higher amount (up to $50) set by a housing authority.[179] The average income of a family receiving federal housing assistance is approximately $12,000.

Under the Section 8 tenant program (called the "Housing Voucher Program"), the housing subsidy is paid directly to the landlord on behalf of the participating family, and then the family pays the difference between the amount of rent charged and the amount of the public voucher. In the program called Section 8 "Project-Based Rental Assistance," funds are provided to owners of housing projects, who then agree to lease units to low-income families at below-market rates. While these programs are administered at the regional, state, and local levels, HUD pays for the subsidies as well as the cost of program administration.[180]

From 2005 to 2010, HUD spending on Section 8 low-income housing assistance programs (both tenant-based and project-based) rose by 18.4 percent, or by 4.3 billion[181]. Increases in the average subsidy per beneficiary account for most of the additional expenditures. The remainder is accounted for by a slight growth in the number of subsidized families (110,000). The budget for public housing has also increased moderately in recent years, reversing the sharp downward trend between 2000 and 2005.[182] However, the permanent removal of public housing units under the HOPE IV program led to growing unmet housing needs among low-income groups.[183] At the same time, investment in the construction of low-income housing spurred by the Low-Income Housing Tax Credit (LIHTC) dried up, since the incentives are a stimulus to developers only when developers are earning profits on which they owe tax. During the Great Recession and the years after, many developers were not earning large enough profits to make tax incentives a significant factor.

Overall, the need for low-income housing assistance continues to outpace the ability of federal, state, and local governments to supply it. In 2005, more than 6.5 million households received housing assistance. This number dropped to 4.9 million in 2009, a 26 percent decline within five years.

Unemployment Insurance (UI)

Perhaps the most obvious form of assistance one would expect during an economic downturn is Unemployment Insurance (UI). Created as part of Franklin Roosevelt's New Deal, UI replaces a fraction of the wages of those who lose their jobs, typically for up to 26 weeks. Responsibility for the program is shared between the federal government and states; the federal government pays for administrative costs, while states are responsible for the actual payments to individuals. State UI programs must abide by a small number of federal guidelines, but, other than that, states have latitude in setting eligibility criteria and benefit levels. Funding for much of UI comes from a payroll tax on employers that is based upon the history of former employees collecting benefits; generally, the more that employees use UI, the more in taxes the employer will pay.

The size of the weekly UI benefit varies widely by state. The benefit is determined as a proportion of the ex-worker's weekly earnings. The most generous states, Hawaii and Rhode Island, cover 54.3 percent and 45.9 percent of lost weekly earnings, respectively, which amounts to an average weekly benefit of $416 and $380, respectively. The least generous states, Mississippi and Florida, cover 29.7 percent and 29.5 percent of lost weekly earnings, respectively, or an average weekly benefit of $190 and $230.[184] Since the cost of living varies significantly across states, these comparisons need to be considered carefully.

Once a person has exhausted 26 weeks of state UI, the federal government provides a basic package of "extended" UI for up to 11 weeks, assuming the state's unemployment problem is severe. Due to the impacts of the Great Recession, a federal emergency fund was created by Congress to provide longer UI extensions than the basic package. The duration of the emergency federal extension also depends on the severity of a state's unemployment problem. The states with the highest rates of unemployment are now receiving 73 additional weeks of UI, for a total of 99 weeks; all states are receiving at least 34 weeks of extended UI from the federal government, or a total of 60 weeks.

Prior to the downturn in 2007, the national unemployment rate hovered around 4.5 percent. During the Great Recession and its aftermath, unemployment rates rose to more than 10 percent and then fell slowly to 8.6 percent by November 2011. As of October 2011, ten states were still experiencing unemployment rates above 10 percent: Nevada (13.4 percent), California (11.7 percent), Michigan (10.6 percent), Mississippi (10.6 percent), South Carolina (10.5 percent), Rhode Island (10.4 percent), North Carolina (10.4 percent), Florida (10.3 percent), Georgia (10.2 percent), and Illinois (10.1 percent).[185]

Given these high rates of joblessness, the number of individuals collecting UI benefits has increased tremendously. At the beginning of 2007, roughly 2.5 million Americans were receiving UI payments. That number rose to 6.6 million in mid-2009. By the end of 2010, just over 4 million of the unemployed were receiving UI and about 6 million are projected to receive UI in 2012.[186]

Not all unemployed workers receive UI payments. During the downturn, only between 30 to 40 percent of unemployed workers received UI. There are a number of reasons for ineligibility and nonparticipation. Although specific rules vary by state, in general, individuals may not receive UI if they have been fired for cause or quit a job. Although some states have modified this requirement, eligibility is also based upon having accrued a certain amount of earnings within a "base period," traditionally counted as the first four of the most recently completed five calendar quarters. Low wage and voluntary part-time workers may not have earned enough money to qualify, particularly if they have had volatility in their employment.[187]

Overall, for people in the bottom 20 percent of the income distribution, UI was a powerful source of income protection during the Great Recession.[188] Between 2008 and 2009 alone, the number of people receiving UI rose 67 percent while the average amount of benefits to those receiving UI grew by 77 percent.[189] However, millions of unemployed workers have already exhausted their UI benefits,[190] and even though Congress extended benefits through the end of 2012, some states have tightened eligibility or shortened the length of benefits offered.[191]

The costs of UI for states and the federal government are substantial. Federal and state spending on UI rose from $33 billion in fiscal year 2007 to a peak of $159 billion in fiscal year 2010. It was estimated to decline to $120 billion in fiscal year 2011, in part due to fewer UI claims in the recovery, but also due to state decisions to reduce the duration of the benefit.

Looking to the future, if federal and state governments do not continue the extensions of UI that originated in the 2009 stimulus, the poverty rate may increase even more rapidly than is now projected. The pace of job growth is not projected to be rapid enough to eliminate, in the near future, the sustained joblessness induced by the Great Recession.[192] On the other hand, passage of the one-year extension of UI, for 2012, was contentious, and it was not clear whether benefits would be extended again.[193]

Earned Income Tax Credit (EITC)

A variety of recent tax-policy changes have helped low-income Americans. The 2009 federal stimulus package expanded the 1997 child tax credit so that a larger number of low-income households receive benefit from the credit.[194] In 2009 and 2010, the new Making Work Pay (MWP) tax credit also provided $400 to individuals and $800 to joint filers. Payroll tax relief enacted by Congress in 2009 benefited the working poor and near poor. On the other hand, relief from the Alternative Minimum Tax, although popular with the public, had little impact on the poor and near poor. Perhaps the key tax reform for working poor families with children is the Earned Income Tax Credit (EITC), which was enacted by Congress in 1975 and expanded four times (1986, 1990, 1993 and 2001).

An EITC is a refundable credit aimed at the lower portion of the income distribution. It is typically received as a lump sum tax rebate, after an income tax form is filed. Many states offer an EITC that is patterned after the federal credit. The federal EITC is designed to reward and supplement earnings while reducing the tax burden of eligible households. For workers with two children at the very low end of the earnings distribution, it gives a credit equal to

$0.40 for every dollar earned.[195] In order to receive any EITC, an individual or household must have some earnings during the calendar year and must file a federal tax return. In other words, the EITC provides no benefit to those who do not work, including those suffering long-term unemployment due to the Great Recession.

The value of the EITC rises as earnings rise, and then flattens out until earnings reach a point where the maximum credit is achieved. The credit then decreases after this point, until it phases out completely. The level of earnings at which these changes occur varies by household size and composition. For example, in 2010, the maximum EITC payment for a mother and three or more children was $5,666, after the household earned $12,590. The value of the household's credit begins to decline when earnings reach $16,450, and the credit is zero when earnings exceed $43,352.[196] The income limits are somewhat higher for households headed by a married couple.

While the EITC is an important tool in federal anti-poverty policy, it responds to recessionary periods in different ways for different families. As a recession occurs, some families are more likely to begin receiving this benefit, while others lose it. For example, the probability of receiving EITC increases for two-income households if one earner loses his/her job. In other words, the loss of one income could decrease total household income enough to make a formerly ineligible household eligible for the EITC. On the other hand, if a single-income head of household becomes unemployed and generates little or no earnings, that family may be less likely to receive an EITC payment, or that payment might be lower than what would be received for working during the full year.

EITC claims have risen by almost 3 million since 2006, from 23 million households to nearly 26 million. While this increase is pronounced, claims had been rising steadily since the mid-1990s. EITC has always enjoyed relatively high participation rates compared to programs that are more administratively burdensome and socially stigmatized. The somewhat sharper increase in EITC claims after the recession began in 2007 was aided by provisions in the 2009 stimulus package that increased the income limit for married couples and for families with three or more children.[197] Total outlays for the EITC increased at a somewhat higher rate than total returns, due to increases in the amount of the credit for qualifying families.

The EITC is probably one of the most politically secure aspects of America's safety net. However, the credit applies only to those who work, and it benefits many non-poor as well as poor households. Consequently, the EITC has historically had substantial bipartisan support in the Congress. If, however, fiscal concerns cause a complete rewrite of the tax code, even the EITC could be at some risk. As we shall see in the next chapter, some states have pared back their own EITCs to help pay for other tax cuts or to help balance the budget.

Multiple Program Participation

We have described the major federal programs that comprise the safety net one at a time, noting that they have somewhat different eligibility requirements and offer different benefits depending on family circumstances. From the perspective of a low-income family, however, there is no single program that will address all of its basic needs. The challenge for the needy is to piece together, where feasible, benefits from multiple programs to help a family make ends meet. In some states and localities, helpful caseworkers or social workers assist needy families in navigating the complexity of the governmental safety net as well as private charities.

In this era of computerization and instant communication, one might expect that there is a single, up-to-date website or other source of information that reports how well the 50 million impoverished Americans are being served by the multiple programs that comprise the safety net. How many low-income families participate in two, three, or four or more safety net programs? How many families access only one program, even though they might be eligible for several? However, there is no such resource quickly available at the national level that documents eligibility for multiple programs or actual participation in multiple programs. One reason for this conundrum is quite simple: A family's eligibility cannot typically be determined until they apply for assistance and their circumstances are measured in light of program eligibility requirements. Even the rate of multiple program participation is an ill-defined concept until we define the precise time periods for consideration (e.g., a certain number of months, a year, or a span of several years).

We can gain some insight into the extent of multiple program participation by looking at data from the Survey of Income and Program Participation (SIPP). The SIPP is overseen by the U.S. Census Bureau. Within each SIPP panel, interviews are conducted every four months to obtain information about each individual in a sampled household for each intervening month between interviews, gathering data on demographics, income sources, public assistance program participation, household and family structure, jobs and work history. Each SIPP panel begins with a new sample. When weighted, the SIPP provides estimates that are nationally representative of households in the U.S.

Table 3 examines multiple program participation in 2006, before the recession, and most recently in 2011. We look at the benefits received from other programs among households that reported receipt of SNAP, TANF, or UI by someone in the household in April of the interview year. Because we are concerned about the most vulnerable families, we limit our examination to households with income 200 percent or less of the federal poverty line.

Looking first at households that received SNAP, we see that nine in ten also report receipt of public health insurance—at least for someone in the household. The proportion who also receive TANF declines between 2006 and 2010, but that is likely due in part to the growing number of individuals entering onto the SNAP rolls during that period who may not have been eligible for TANF; if we look at households who received TANF, the proportion also receiving SNAP remains about the same in 2006 and 2010. Not surprisingly, the proportion of SNAP households who also receive unemployment benefits increases over time, although just 8.5 percent of SNAP households get UI as well. In both time periods, about 14–15 percent of these households also received UI, and between 25 and 30 percent received Section 8 assistance or lived in public housing.

Turning to households that receive TANF, nearly all also have someone in the house who receives public health insurance. This is not surprising, since generally most TANF recipients are also eligible for Medicaid. Very few of these households receive UI benefits. Since UI benefits are counted as income in determining eligibility for TANF, most households that receive UI would not be "poor

Table 3. Multiple Program Participation Among Low-Income Households.

	2006 (%)	2011 (%)
SNAP Households Receiving:		
TANF	20.5	13.4
UI	3.5	8.5
SSI	15.8	13.7
Housing Assistance	30.0	25.2
Public Health Insurance	93.0	91.6
TANF Households Receiving:		
SNAP	90.5	92.5
UI	0.9	2.3
SSI	26.4	23.7
Housing Assistance	37.6	36.4
Public Health Insurance	99.5	96.9
UI Households Receiving:		
SNAP	38.6	49.8
TANF	2.3	2.0
SSI	<1.0	4.9
Housing Assistance	11.3	8.5
Public Health Insurance	69.5	70.9

Source: Tabulations of data from the *Survey of Income and Program Participation* compiled by Luke Shaefer, School of Social Work, University of Michigan.

enough" to also receive TANF. Approximately a quarter of TANF households also have at least one household member receiving SSI, and just under two-fifths received some sort of housing assistance. Although these proportions (with the exception of UI) are smaller than the numbers reported with SNAP households, TANF is a much smaller program than SNAP.

Unemployment Insurance is not a means-tested program, so we might not expect to see as much multiple program participation. A smaller proportion of these households receive SNAP, although that proportion grew from 38.6 percent to 49.8 percent over the course of the recession. About 70 percent receive public health insurance during this time period, and relatively few of these households receive other benefits.

The Future of the Safety Net

In the next chapter, we explain why the federal government and the states are under budgetary pressures to reduce spending on the safety net. Since the partial safety net is comprised of a variety of distinct programs with somewhat different legislative advocates and degrees of public appeal, it is unlikely that the United States Congress would seek to trim, overhaul, or modernize the entire safety net in a single piece of legislation. More likely, what will unfold is a series of incremental modifications to the safety net over the next decade, or until the governmental budgets are placed on a sustainable path.

In the political deliberations that will unfold, we expect that the welfare of low-income populations will be at considerable risk. By offering this unsettling prediction, we are not suggesting that elected officials are cruel or uncaring. In order to appreciate the dilemma of elected officials and the citizens who elect them, the fiscal challenges of the country must be appreciated.

5
Risks to the Safety Net in the Aftermath of the Great Recession

In 2009–2011, President Obama and the U.S. Congress took major steps aimed at bolstering the safety net during and soon after the Great Recession. The $787 billion stimulus package of 2009 contained a temporary burst of spending for safety net programs while the federal debt-ceiling agreement of 2011 was designed to shield the largest safety-net programs from an initial round of automatic cuts to defense and domestic spending.

Looking forward, however, it appears that the safety net is far from secure. Since the U.S. economy is unlikely to reach full employment (less than 5 percent) until 2017 (or even the end of the decade) and since tens of millions of Americans living near the poverty line have much diminished levels of savings and assets due to the Great Recession, the need for safety net programs is likely to remain quite large between now and 2020.[198] During this same period, while revenues to the federal government and state governments will be rising gradually due to the slow recovery, politicians will be under increasing pressure to curb government spending in order to avoid or curb deficits and reduce the large accumulated debt. Some states will enact new sources of revenue, but the enactment of substantial new sources of revenue by the federal government is not likely to be politically appealing to members of Congress and their constituents.

In this chapter, we explore a variety of ways that the safety net is already being threatened and may be cut further in the next decade. We set the stage by describing how the 2009 stimulus package gave a temporary boost to the safety net. Using surveys from the Federal Reserve Board, we then consider how well low-income people were doing in 2010 compared to 2007. We then describe the 2011 debt-ceiling agreement and the strengths and weaknesses of the safety-net protections that are contained in this agreement. We then describe a variety of ways that federal and state governments are already reducing spending on the safety net and thereby placing low-income populations at risk. These early cuts provide an indication of more substantial and widespread cuts that are likely in the years ahead, unless the economy recovers much more rapidly than expected.

The Recovery Act of 2009

By early 2009, it was becoming increasingly clear that the Great Recession was even worse than expected. The Obama administration and the Congress responded with the temporary, $787 billion American Reinvestment and Recovery Act. The main purpose of the Recovery Act (also called the "federal stimulus" package for short) was to soften the impact of the downturn, accelerate the economic recovery, and create jobs for Americans. The stimulus package, while huge in absolute size, was actually a compromise between those who argued that a much larger stimulus (say, $1 trillion) was advisable and those who questioned whether any stimulus was likely to be effective enough to justify an exacerbation of the bleak federal fiscal situation.

Economists will debate for many years the precise impact of the 2009 stimulus package, but it appears that the temporary package "worked in the sense that the recession would have been substantially worse without the stimulus."[199] But even with the stimulus, the economy was left "badly injured."[200] It is less clear how the slow economic recovery since June 2009 has been affected (positively or negatively) by the fiscal policies of the U.S. federal government. It may take scholars many years to answer that question, and even today there are debates about whether the actions of Congress during the Roosevelt administration helped or hurt America's recovery from the Great Depression. Economics is a science but a very imperfect one.

What we can say with confidence is that, in the design of the stimulus package, the President and Congress made a special effort to channel substantial amounts of funds to low-income families and depressed communities.[201] A case can be made that all of the $787 billion helped boost the recovery and thereby mitigated some of the hardships incurred by the poor and near poor, but roughly $240 billion of the stimulus package was aimed directly at helping low-income people, largely through spending in safety net programs.[202]

Table 4 provides an itemized accounting of the portions of the stimulus package directed specifically at low-income people. The largest single portion ($87.1 billion) went to the states to cushion the rising costs of Medicaid. Other stimulus funds helped bolster specific programs in the safety net (e.g., Medicaid, SNAP, TANF, and HUD housing assistance, the Earned Income Tax Credit, Unemployment Insurance, assistance in payment of energy bills, child care, and support for public schools in low-income communities).

Tracking the Family Finances of Low-Income Americans

The Great Recession and its aftermath, coupled with the responses of policy makers at the federal, state, and local levels of government (including the Recovery Act), have had a wide range of impacts on low-income Americans. Unfortunately, there is no single indicator that one can consult to determine how low-income Americans are doing after the Great Recession (and in light of the policy responses to the recession) compared to how they were doing before the Great Recession. An important indicator, however, is family finances of low-income Americans, which are now surveyed regularly by social scientists affiliated with the U.S. Federal Reserve System.

The two key measures tracked by the Fed are a family's net worth (assets minus liabilities) and "cash income." Although the Fed's definition of income is somewhat different than some of the income definitions we reviewed in Chapter 2, it is broad enough to capture the

Table 4. Portions of the $787 Billion Temporary Stimulus Program Aimed Specifically at Low-Income Populations.

Program	Estimated Costs (billions)
Medicaid Assistance to the States	87.1
Expanded Unemployment Compensation	35.8
Subsidized health insurance premiums for the jobless	25.1
Expanded Food Assistance	20.9
Expanded Child Tax Credit for filers with incomes btwn $3k and $12K	14.8
Grants to Public Schools in Low-Income Areas	13.0
Redevelopment of Distressed Areas	6.5
Insulation for Low-Income Families	5.0
Exempt Unemployment Insurance benefits from Federal Tax	4.7
Increase the Earned Income Tax Credit	4.7
Modernize the Unemployment Insurance System	4.2
Upgrade Public Housing Units	4.0
TANF Assistance for States	2.7
Remove Lead-Based Paint from Housing	2.4
Head Start and Early Head Start	2.1
Section 8 Housing Subsidies	2.0
Child Care for Low-Income Families	2.0
Renovations at Community Health Centers	2.0
Housing Assistance for the Homeless	1.5
Temporary Coverage for Medicaid Ineligibles	1.3
Subsidize Medicare Premiums for Low-Income Individuals	0.6
Meals/Transport for Low-Income Children	0.1

Source: Farhana Hossain, Amanda Cox, John McGrath, Stephen Weitberg, "The Stimulus Plan: How to Spend $787 Billion," *New York Times*, November 15, 2009.

main effects of the Great Recession on market income and some of the effects of government transfer programs. In particular, the Fed's family income measure includes wages, self-employment and business income, taxable and tax exempt interest income, dividends, realized capital gains, food stamps and other government transfers (excluding Medicaid and Medicare), and pensions and withdrawals from retirement savings. Income is measured before taxes, and thus does not account for the Earned Income Tax Credit and other tax provisions or the amount of taxes paid by families. All measures of income and net worth are adjusted for inflation.

In one study, Fed analysts interviewed the same sample of families twice in order to determine how family finances changed from 2007 to 2009. They achieved an impressive re-interview rate of 89 percent. A limitation of this survey is that 2009 is too early to capture much of the impact of the Great Recession on long-term unemployment or the full impact of the federal stimulus program and other policy responses.[203]

In a second study, Fed analysts compared the family finances of a representative sample of American families in 2007 to the family finances of a representative sample of American families in 2010.[204] This study does not have advantage of re-interviewing the same families, but it adds an additional year, 2010, and it is based on large samples of families in both years.

In the first study, Fed analysts found that median family income dropped slightly from $50,100 in 2007 to $49,800 in 2009. However, median family income in the bottom 40 percent of the distribution rose while it declined in the upper 60 percent of the distribution. The most adversely affected families were at the top ten percent of the income distribution, where median income declined from $216,800 to $187,300, a drop of 14.4 percent in two years. The median family income in the bottom 20 percent of the distribution rose from $13,600 to $16,800, an increase of 18.5 percent.

The authors indicate that the composition of the bottom 20 percent of the income distribution changed in this sample of families. Of those who were in the bottom 20 percent in 2009, 64.9 percent were also in the bottom 20 percent in 2007. But 19.1 percent of the families came from the second quintile, 6.7 percent came from the third quintile, 3.0 percent came from the fourth quintile, and 1.9 percent came from the upper quintile. In a subanalysis of those families that were in the bottom quintile in both 2007 and 2009, the authors showed that their median net worth declined from about $10,000 to $4,500.

During this period, it is important to recognize that average housing values dropped substantially while the major stock market indices dropped by almost 50 percent (from 9/07 to 3/09). But the full impact of the Great Recession on the unemployment rate (especially long-term unemployment) and the poverty rate had not yet occurred. And real GDP did not return to its pre-recession levels until the third quarter of 2011. As a result, we should not be surprised that the net worth of these families was more adversely affected than their incomes. The median (mean) net worth among the families declined from $125,000 ($595,000) in 2007 to $96,000 ($481,000) in 2009, as about 63 percent of families reported a decline in their net worth.

The Fed analysts found that median net worth declined in all income groups, although the percentage of families reporting a decline in net worth was somewhat larger (65–71 percent) in the higher-income groups than in the lower-income groups (58–63 percent). In the lowest 20 percent and highest 20 percent of the income distribution, however, the median decline in net worth was around 18 percent. The drop was actually slightly larger (-21 percent) in the middle of the income distribution, where housing is a dominant contributor to family assets.

In the second study, the basic finding was that median (mean) real family income declined 7.7 percent (11.1 percent), suggesting that adverse labor market outcomes were beginning to be felt. The only subgroups of families that did not experience a drop in income were retirees and other nonworking families. The income declines were most pronounced among highly educated families, those with household heads under the age of 55, and families living in the West and Southwest of the U.S.

When the changes were broken down by income groups, only one subgroup did not experience a decline in family income: those families in the bottom 20 percent of the income distribution. Among those families, median (mean) family income was $12,900 ($12,900) in 2007 and $13,400 ($12,900) in 2010. A subanalysis by the Fed analysts reveals that low-income families did experience a wage decline, but they also experienced an increase in government transfer payments. This is suggestive evidence that the governmental safety net was doing its job.

Since the low-income group may include some families with substantial net worth, it is also instructive to look at what happened to the incomes of families toward the bottom of the wealth distribution. Among families in the bottom quartile (25 percent) of the wealth distribution, median family income dropped from $24,600 in 2007 to $23,700 in 2010, while mean family income increased from $30,500 in 2007 to $32,600 in 2010.

Americans in the middle of the wealth distribution took the largest relative decline in family income. For families in the third quartile of the net worth distribution, median (mean) family income dropped from $59,500 ($69,800) in 2007 to $54,900 ($63,300) in 2010. The drop in family income at the very top of the wealth distribution was smaller. For families in the top ten percent of the wealth distribution, median (mean) family income declined from $165,500 ($364,200) in 2007 to $163,200 ($297,900) in 2010.

In summary, it is too early to draw firm conclusions because data on family finances have only been analyzed through 2010. Certainly more research is needed to determine how the well-being of low-wealth, low-income families has been affected by the Great Recession, including the families who became poor for the first time due to long-term unemployment. It does appear, however, that many low-income Americans—thanks in part to the safety set and the conscious responses of government—were able to hold their fragile finances together through the Great Recession and perhaps 18 months thereafter.

Our thesis is that a big risk for low-income families—possibly bigger than the risk faced in the 2007–2010 period—is during the slow recovery through the end of the decade. As we shall see, there are already some signs that elected officials may begin to reduce financial support for the safety net before the economy has fully recovered. Once the federal stimulus package expired and the funds were expended, the political discussion began to focus on the need for fiscal austerity. The earliest signs of trouble occurred in 2010 during the national debate over whether the debt-ceiling should be raised.

The 2011 Debt-Ceiling Agreement: Protections of the Safety Net

The federal budget deficit was $1.3 trillion in fiscal year 2010 and was projected to be $1.6 trillion in fiscal year 2011 and $1.1 trillion in fiscal year 2012.[205] The $1.6 trillion figure, expressed as a share of Gross Domestic Product, represents 10.9 percent, the largest share since World War II.[206] Concern about the huge size of these deficits and their long-term impact on the economy and younger Americans have politicians of both parties looking at new ways to restrain federal spending.

As part of the July 2011 Congressional agreement to raise the federal debt ceiling, a bipartisan agreement was reached to enact two rounds of savings in federal spending. Together, the two rounds were intended to trim $2.1 trillion from federal budget deficits from fiscal year 2012 to fiscal year 2021.[207]

In round 1, $900 billion of projected spending growth will be trimmed from the federal budget during the next decade. These savings are accomplished in the form of caps on growth in discretionary programs that otherwise would have occurred due to inflation. Separate caps are applied to discretionary defense ("security") and non-defense spending. In other words, the real (inflation-adjusted) expenditures on these discretionary programs will decline steadily for ten years.

A 50–50 split between defense and non-defense savings is required only for the first two years. There are concerns that, over time, a larger share of the savings will be squeezed from non-defense programs.[208] For example, if elected officials find it more politically expedient after the first two years to make cuts to non-defense accounts than defense accounts, then programs for low-income populations—which fall under the non-defense accounts—may experience even deeper cuts.

Low-income populations are somewhat shielded from the first round of savings because entitlement programs (such as SNAP, SSI, and Medicaid) are not subject to the caps and some other low-income programs (e.g., TANF) are also exempt from the caps.[209] There are, however, a variety of discretionary programs for low-income populations that are not shielded from cuts. They include at least the following programs and/or services that are supported with federal funds: housing assistance; Head Start; child care assistance programs; job training assistance; a nutrition program for Women, Infants and Children (WIC); Meals on Wheels for the elderly; family planning services; community health centers; services for special education students; financial assistance for college students; and energy-bill assistance for low-income families.[210]

Fully a third of the non-defense spending that is subject to the new federal spending caps is funding provided to the states for education, infrastructure, and other programs and services. Once states realize that fewer federal funds will be received, state politicians will be looking to cut back programs, and some programs for low-income populations are likely to be targeted.[211]

In round 2 of the 2011 debt-ceiling agreement, an additional $1.2 trillion in savings will occur automatically because a bipartisan committee in Congress was unable to achieve consensus on its own fiscal plan. The automatic reductions are to be spread evenly over the fiscal years from 2013 to 2021. Half of the savings are slated to come from defense and half from non-defense spending.[212]

As in the first round of savings, key low-income assistance programs (SNAP, Medicaid, and TANF) are exempt from cuts. But the same discretionary programs that are vulnerable in round 1 are vulnerable again in round 2. And the agreement specifies that the automatic reductions will be accomplished by applying a uniform percentage cut to all unprotected programs except for Medicare, which cannot be cut more than 2 percent.[213]

The automatic cuts in round 2 may also complicate implementation of the new health care reform law, particularly programs that begin in 2014. There are discretionary federal funds that are necessary to administer and implement the new law, yet these funds will be subject to automatic cuts in round 2.[214]

Whether the automatic cuts will actually occur remains an open question. Key members of Congress (e.g., Senator John McCain of Arizona) and the Obama administration (Secretary of Defense Leon Panetta) have signaled that the automatic cuts aimed at defense are not tolerable.[215] Congress has until January 2013 to make adjustments before the automatic cuts begin to take effect. If Congress shifts more of the cuts from the defense sector to the non-defense sector of the budget, programs aimed at low-income populations may be placed at even greater risk of cuts than they are under the current agreement.

Perhaps most at risk will be discretionary federal spending programs that boost the fiscal positions of state and local governments. About one-third of non-security discretionary spending by the federal government is distributed to state and local governments. Any federal actions that squeeze the states may result, indirectly, in state cutbacks in the safety net.[216] This indirect harm to the safety net is already occurring due to general fiscal pressures on state and local governments.

Examples of Cuts to Discretionary Programs

Some of the consequences of federal spending reductions have already begun to become apparent.. For example, the largest food-relief group in America, Feeding America, works through 200 food banks to serve 37 million hungry Americans with 3.3 billion pounds of food. About a quarter of the food comes from the U.S. Department of Agriculture in the form of commodities. Federal spending cuts in 2012 over 2011 levels at USDA have reduced commodity donations to food banks by 45 percent. Feeding America, which does not receive any government money for operating support, scrambled to fill the unexpected loss of commodities through greater levels of philanthropy.[217]

Meanwhile, federal assistance for Advanced Placement courses in high schools was reduced from $43 million in 2011 to $27 million in 2012. Low-income students, who were exempt from AP exam fees for decades, have to pay $15 each for the first three AP exams they take, and $53 per exam for any AP exam beyond that. (The full fee is $87 per exam for students from middle class and wealthy families). As a result of the new fees, it was projected that 29,000 fewer low-income students would take the AP exams in the spring of 2012 and thus these students would enter college with fewer college credits and face higher costs of college completion.[218]

College students also face reductions in federal assistance for the costs of their tuition and living expenses. Pell grants, which provide assistance to lower-income college students, were retained at a maximum level of $5,550 per student. But grants for summer school were eliminated and tighter eligibility requirements resulted in at least 125,000 of the 10 million recipients losing their grants.[219] Congress took temporary action to protect eight million college students from an automatic increase in the interest rate on subsidized loans to low- and middle-income college students under the Stafford loan program, delaying an increase in the rate for new loans made after June 30, 2012.[220] Graduate students faced a new burden: a requirement to pay the interest on their accumulated educational debt while still in school.[221]

Thus, the practical effect of the 2011 debt-ceiling agreement was to place greater budgetary pressure on safety-net programs that were not protected from automatic cuts. We shall argue in Chapter 6 that there are wiser methods of making cuts to the safety net, even accepting the proposition that cuts are necessary. But the 2011 agreement was only the beginning of what is likely to be a multi-year process of fiscal decisions aimed at bringing the budget of the federal government into balance.

Even programs such as SNAP, which were supposed to be protected by the debt-ceiling deal, may not be fully protected. Both the House and Senate versions of the 2012 Farm Bill contain cuts to SNAP spending, although the Senate version contained far fewer cuts than the House version. The Senate version is of particular interest because its cuts to SNAP spending received a substantial number of votes from Senators of both political parties. While the Senate bill reauthorized SNAP for a projected $768 billion over ten years, about $4.5 billion over ten years was saved by placing additional limits on who could receive SNAP assistance and by reducing by $90 per month the average SNAP benefit for 500,000 households.[222]

Concerns about "Waste, Fraud, and Abuse" in the Safety Net

Safety net programs may also be at risk of spending reductions due to concerns about waste, fraud, and abuse. Even though evidence does not exist of widespread abuse or fraud taking place in the administration of safety net programs, isolated incidents of such abuse often receive great media attention. These programs are also vulnerable to being placed under the auditor's microscope because their beneficiaries are not politically potent.

A revealing feature of the 2011 debt-ceiling agreement was its treatment of "fraud and abuse" in the safety net. Safeguards in the 2011 agreement were applied to "program integrity" expenditures in both income security and health care programs, thereby blocking any cuts to funds used for the purpose of discovering fraud and abuse in the safety net, thereby ensuring that only those who are truly eligible for assistance receive it.

Even though the spending on (and savings from) program-integrity measures were projected to be small relative to the trillion-dollar size of the 2011 agreement, Congress was determined to protect efforts to prevent or correct "overpayment" in the safety net.[223] The implication of this agreement is that efforts to reduce "waste, fraud, and abuse" in the safety net are seen as having a political or symbolic value that is greater than the modest accounting value of the anticipated savings.

For nearly all of the safety net, mismanagement of programs and administrative errors—as opposed to fraud by program recipients—is the main cause of erroneous spending. For example, the U.S. Department of Labor (DOL) estimates that the annual overpayment rate in UI is about 11.6 percent, which means that about $1 out of $9 is improperly expended.[224] The principal reason for overpayments is that some beneficiaries continue to receive assistance for a period of time after they have found employment. However, DOL estimates that most of this improper payment is because of errors made by agency employees and not by UI recipients who are deliberately defrauding the government.

Medicaid has been deemed a "high-risk program" from a fiscal perspective because of the known frequency of improper payments and a history of inadequate fiscal oversight.[225] Medicare and Medicaid together are estimated to make about $70 billion per year in improper payments. Fraud in these programs has been the subject of recent Congressional hearings in both the House and Senate, although most of the fraud is perpetrated by providers and not by beneficiaries. Conservative groups pressed for more serious measures to reduce waste, fraud and abuse,[226] while the Obama administration took stronger administrative actions to reduce waste, fraud, and abuse in Medicaid.[227]

Isolated occurrences of fraud, though, have received media attention, including reports of high-asset individuals receiving SNAP and UI. Efforts to buttress asset tests in federal food assistance, remove millionaires from Unemployment Insurance, and the "program-integrity" provisions of the 2011 debt-ceiling agreement are all examples of efforts designed to stem waste, fraud, and abuse of public programs. Elected officials are becoming increasingly sensitive about newspaper reports that some recipients of cash benefits do not expend the entire benefit on basic family needs. Ten states have enacted laws that prohibit TANF recipients from using welfare dollars to purchase liquor, cigarettes, or guns or to spend their benefits in strip clubs or casinos. Other states have considered similar legislation.

The state laws come on the heels of a new federal law (2010) that compels all states, by 2014, to prevent TANF recipients from using their benefits at liquor stores, casinos, and adult entertainment businesses. Although such restrictions are quite difficult to enforce, the states are now, in theory, vulnerable to a potential loss of federal funds if they do not establish and implement such policies. In Massachusetts, for example, recipients are required to pay back the misused money while store owners can be fined up to $1,000 for accepting money. If it is shown that cash welfare recipients and store owners ignore these new laws, then a public backlash against anti-poverty programs could occur. Critics point out that these efforts play into the worst stereotypes of poor people.[228]

In summary, while mismanagement problems appear to play a larger role in erroneous spending than does fraud by recipients, concerns about waste, fraud, and abuse need to be handled carefully. If not, there is risk that elected officials will respond hastily with reforms of the safety net that inadvertently put needy Americans at additional risk. In other words, without public confidence that the safety net is targeting the truly needy in society, public support for cuts in the safety net is likely to grow.

State and Local Cutbacks of the Safety Net

As the U.S. economy began to enter a slow recovery after June 2009, tax revenues to state governments climbed for six consecutive quarters and were expected to continue their climb through 2012 and beyond. Due to the slow rate of growth, state revenues in 2011 remained 6 percent below their 2008 level, or 11 percent lower after inflation is taken into account.[229] States are under intense pressure to help local governments, which face persistent fiscal problems due to a sharp decline in housing values, the loss of property tax revenue, and the multi-year lag between changes in housing values and changes in property tax revenues. Moreover, many states face long-term, structural fiscal problems as well as short-term crises related to the Great Recession. One recent study found that Illinois, New Jersey, California, Virginia, New York, and Virginia have unfunded pension liabilities for public workers ranging from $1,835 to $2,882 per resident. The combination of rising pension liabilities and unchecked Medicaid spending has some states facing persistent fiscal crisis, even if the economy recovers fully and quickly.[230]

Looking forward to the 2013–2020 period when the economy may gradually recover to full employment, it is important to realize that many states have already coped with three bad fiscal years (2009–2011), partly by spending down what were once healthy levels of cash reserves. Many states are required by their constitutions to achieve balanced budgets.[231] The 2009 federal stimulus dollars, which were extremely helpful to state and local governments on a temporary basis, have also been expended. Since tax increases are not a likely response of politicians, it is probable that low-income populations face more unfavorable changes to state spending and tax policies during the remainder of the decade.[232] On the spending side of the ledger, states have tried to restrain nonessential expenditures in a variety of areas while making significant cuts in spending on education (K-12 and higher education) and criminal justice. Layoffs of state and local employees blunted some of the impact of the federal stimulus spending while partially offsetting some encouraging signs of employment growth in the private sector. About 611,000 jobs were lost in the state and local government sector since that sector's peak employment was recorded in September 2008, and more layoffs of government employees are predicted.[233]

The explosive growth of Medicaid spending creates a persistent, worrisome gap between projected spending and projected revenues in many states.[234] The 2009 stimulus package provided states two years of relief from Medicaid costs ($90 billion in enhanced Medicaid payments plus $55 billion in general fiscal support), but once those monies were expended they were not replaced.

Since household incomes remain depressed from the Great Recession, elected officials in most states are reluctant to consider general tax increases. Consequently, states are looking aggressively for additional spending reductions, and programs that serve the poor and near poor are at risk of significant cuts. Numerous programs are vulnerable to spending reductions by governors and state legislators, but some of the most likely to see cuts are as follows.

Reducing Medicaid Spending

For many states, Medicaid is the fastest-growing program in the state budget, yet much of what states spend on Medicaid is required by the federal government in the complex partnership defined by the U.S. Congress. Fearing that states might choose to balance their budgets by curbing eligibility for Medicaid or changing enrollment procedures, Congress actually prohibited such cost-saving measures until the scheduled Medicaid expansion—accompanied by more federal spending on Medicaid—occurs in 2014. Given the constraints they face, states take different approaches to curbing the growth of Medicaid spending.

Arizona is one of 39 states that has cut the rates that health care providers are allowed to charge under the state Medicaid program.[235] While reducing payments to providers can result in significant savings in the short run, some providers respond by refusing to treat Medicaid patients, and lower reimbursement rates will only exacerbate this problem. For fiscal year 2012, 46 states reported that they planned to lower provider rates. But this strategy is a stop-gap measure. Starting in 2014, under the federal health-care law, Medicaid programs will be required by federal law to pay the same rates for services as the Medicare program—rates that are much more generous to providers and more costly to the government.

A different approach, followed already by 18 states, is to eliminate or reduce optional services such as dental care while implementing new procedures to control expenditures on costly items such as prescription drugs and medical devices.[236] A related approach is greater use of disease and care management, as well as primary care coordinated care, to help achieve more cost-effectiveness with high-cost and high-need patients.

In some states, Medicaid is seen as part of a fiscal emergency. In 2012 the governor of Illinois called for $2.7 billion in Medicaid savings in the next fiscal year, given that Illinois was one of the most indebted states in the country. Illinois has the largest unfunded pension liability in the country ($83 billion as of June 2012), has more than $8 billion in unpaid bills, and is rated second-worst in the country (with only California ranked lower) for creditworthiness by Fitch and Standard and Poor's Rating Services. Illinois established a working group of legislators to reconsider all aspects of the Medicaid program (who is eligible, what services are provided, and how they are paid for) to "save the entire program from collapse."[237]

The governor of Illinois did not get all he asked for, but a $1.6-billion Medicaid austerity plan was enacted. Coverage for chiropractic care was eliminated, while coverage for podiatry was limited to treatment for diabetics. Adult vision care was limited to one pair of eyeglasses every two years. Patient co-payments were added for prescription drugs, especially brand-name drugs. Provider payments to hospitals and nursing homes were reduced. And an estimated 25,000 working parents were removed from coverage as the income limits were reduced from 400 percent of the poverty line to 133 percent of the poverty line. The need for deeper Medicaid cuts was moderated by enactment of a larger cigarette tax. [238]

In Alabama policy makers cut $68 million out of the state's $648 million Medicaid budget in one year. The result were limits on adult coverage of eye care (new glasses no longer covered once every three years, and eye exams covered once every three years instead of two) and prescription drugs (a new limit of one brand drug per month and limits on drugs for coughs and colds).[239]

Governor Jerry Brown of California took a different approach in negotiating with the California legislature over an austerity plan for health spending. The plan called for eliminating the state's child health insurance program, Healthy Families, and enlarging Medi-Cal, the state's version of Medicaid. Savings are expected to occur in at least two ways: the provider reimbursement rates were higher under Healthy Families than under Medi-Cal, and the income tests for eligibility were more generous under Healthy Families (up to $56,000 per year) than under Medi-Cal (up to $30,000 per year).

There may also be some administrative savings in the shift of 880,000 children into Medi-Cal.[240]

Although some of these austerity measures may have merit, we argue in Chapter 6 that a more coherent approach to Medicaid reform is appropriate. In particular, we argue that new models of care for Medicaid patients can reduce spending while improving patient care and health outcomes.

Cuts in Direct and Indirect Cash Assistance

Since states spend a greater amount on cash welfare than the federal government does, fiscally strapped states are beginning to focus on spending for cash-assistance programs. The methods include tighter eligibility requirements, shorter durations of eligibility, and smaller benefit levels.[241] Here are some recent examples of state-level budgetary actions that are aimed at reducing spending on the safety net for low-income populations.

California's TANF program was slated for $3.5 billion in cuts in 2011 as a result of state budget shortfalls. Those savings were to be accomplished by reducing the average cash payment by $3,100 per year, reducing the maximum number of months a beneficiary may be in the program (from 60 to 48 months), and lowering the income threshold for eligibility (from $1,651 to $1,369 per month).[242] In 2012, Governor Brown proposed a second round of cuts to help close the state's $15.7 billion budget deficit. In Brown's agreement with the legislature, the state's welfare-to-work program (called CalWORKS) reduced the period a recipient can receive cash assistance without working from four to two years. Funding for child care assistance was also reduced by 8.7 percent, reducing the number of slots by 10,600. Additional cuts may be necessary if voters do not approve the tax increases that Governor Brown has proposed. [243]

In Arizona, which was hit hard by the Great Recession, policy makers moved away from cash assistance—despite the rising numbers of women and children in need—in favor of other human services programs such as foster care and adoption services. Only about one-third of the federal monies that Arizona received (a total of $200 million per year) were devoted to TANF purposes (direct cash assistance and job training).[244]

California and Arizona are not alone among states that reduced the number of people receiving TANF after the onset of the Great Recession. A total of 16 states tightened TANF eligibility rules, shortened the time limits for receipt of benefits and reduced average benefit levels.[245]

Unemployment compensation was also a target in some states. Florida, Michigan and Missouri reduced the duration of state unemployment benefits that are made available to laid-off workers.[246]

Even in their tax policy changes, which one might think would focus on businesses and high-income individuals, some states have made reforms that will adversely affect low-income populations. Both Michigan and Wisconsin scaled back the state-level Earned Income Tax Credit provisions in their tax codes, reforms that increase state revenue at the expense of the working poor and near poor.[247] Reducing state-earned income credits may be more appealing to elected state officials than imposing broader tax increases on more affluent voters or businesses.

In summary, the welfare of low-income populations is determined by the decisions of state and local governments as well as the decisions of the federal government. And the fiscal conditions of the three levels of government are interdependent, which means that the financial burdens of the safety net may be caught up in political disputes among the three levels of government. The harsh reality is that cutbacks to the safety net by individual states or localities are unlikely to receive the kind of national attention that might occur if the federal government were to consider a major reduction of the safety net. Thus, when federal politicians enact "safeguards" for the safety net but then shift general fiscal burdens to the states, it is not unreasonable for skeptics to argue that the federal government is engaged in a form of deception. In order to have confidence that the interests of low-income populations are protected, it is crucial to track what is happening at state and local levels of government and in the philanthropic sector as well as the more visible federal government.

6
Policy Options for Strengthening the Safety Net

The Great Recession was so deep and lengthy, and the recovery so slow, that the number of people in America who are poor has reached the highest level—almost 50 million—since the official poverty statistic was established in the 1960s. The cruel reality is that poverty continued to increase in America for many months after the Great Recession ended in June 2009.

The monthly rate of job creation after June 2009 was uneven. While the unemployment rate in mid-2012 is down to about 8 percent from a peak of more than 10 percent, millions of Americans have been out of work for six months or more. If current average rates of job creation continue, it will take 88 months to attain the peak level of employment achieved in January 2008, prior to the onset of the Great Recession.[248] The much longer recovery period compared to the recessions of the 1980s and 1990s is not surprising, since the Great Recession had its roots in financial crises, which are known to induce deep recessions with slow recoveries.

As a result, the poverty rate may continue to increase before it begins a slow fall. One of the best indicators of trends in poverty is the monthly count of SNAP (Food Stamp) recipients, and it did not fall for two consecutive months until early 2012.[249] Some estimates suggest that, depending on how anemic the recovery is, the count of SNAP recipients may not begin to decline on a full-year basis until 2014.[250]

The good news is that the U.S. safety net, coupled with some timely stimulus policies, cushioned the impact of the Great Recession, making it less harmful (especially for low-income Americans) than it otherwise would have been. To be sure, not all components of the safety net worked equally well. Federal food assistance, unemployment compensation, Supplemental Security Income, and Medicaid responded robustly to the swelling number of impoverished Americans, but TANF and federal housing programs were not responsive to the brutal force of the Great Recession. One of America's best anti-poverty measures, the Earned Income Tax Credit, was hampered because many low-income people could not find work and thus could not benefit from the program, which is based on earnings.

A slow recovery poses a big risk for low-income Americans because the rate of improvement in the supply of jobs—and the corresponding decline of poverty through increased earnings, occurs at a slower pace compared to the speed at which certain elected officials wish to make cuts to the safety net. Concerns about the federal fiscal situation, coupled with the empty coffers of many state governments, ensure that the safety net will be at risk of cuts in each budgetary deliberation between now and 2020.

Philanthropic donations aimed at low-income families declined at precisely the time that they may have been needed the most: in 2008–2009, during the depths of the recession. However, philanthropy began its recovery (2010–2011) in time to offset some of the recent cuts in the governmental safety net. During the 2013–2020 period, many more families are likely to be looking for private support, since their unemployment compensation may expire and the push for austerity may constrain the amount of support available from government.

In this chapter, we offer a number of options for policy makers to consider that could assist low-income families. We begin with near-term options to protect vulnerable people during the slow recovery from the Great Recession. Our recommendations include: (1) indexing the federal minimum wage for inflation and (2) finding efficiencies in the safety net. In the latter category we discuss reforms to

Medicaid, improving targeting of federal transfer programs, and modifications to non-poverty policies and programs so that low-income individuals receive more benefits. Before presenting our suggestions, we first review what might be considered typical conservative and liberal approaches to these reforms before presenting a policy that might be palatable to both parties. We then look ahead and propose policy options applicable to future downturns in the business cycle. Our recommendations here include reforms to TANF and the unemployment compensation systems, subsidized employment and job training opportunities for those who cannot quickly find new employment, and transforming more of the safety net into a form of automatic fiscal stabilization. The latter recommendation is intended to better manage the business cycle while also helping low-income families.

As a practical constraint on the range of near-term policy options, we explore only options that seem to have some substantive promise (i.e., will help low-income people), as well as some potential for attracting "cross-over" support from elected officials in both political parties. The polarization of American politics often precludes enactment of "bipartisan" measures, which we define as measures that might garner support from the leaders of both political parties in Congress. Instead, a more modest objective is "cross-partisan" support, which we define—following the work of political scientist Charles Jones—as virtually unified political support from one party as well as a limited number of supporters from the opposing party (usually not the leadership).[251] In particular, we offer policy options that might be capable of reaching the 60-vote threshold in the United States Senate—the number necessary to overcome a filibuster threat—in circumstances where the two parties have balanced strength (e.g., a 50–50 partisan mix of the two parties in the Senate). In other words, and despite our individual preferences, if we could not imagine at least ten United States senators from both parties supporting a policy measure, we have not discussed it in any depth in this chapter.

We suspect that many of the grand anti-poverty policies that attract interest among conservative and liberal scholars in the U.S. are unlikely to pass the cross-partisan feasibility test. Indeed, in writing this chapter, both of us recognized that some of the policy reforms we support individually would not meet this standard. For example, we cannot envision a scenario in the foreseeable future where ten Democratic senators would vote for a plan to revamp Social Security as an anti-poverty program by implementing means-testing (like SNAP), as a way of easing fiscal pressures to cut other safety net programs. Likewise, we cannot imagine that ten Republican senators would support enactment of a uniform social insurance system along the model of many Western European countries. Consequently, our focus here is on policy options that are not only palatable to each of us as authors with diverging views but, more importantly, might be politically feasible in the United States Congress, even though we recognize that politics in the U.S. is becoming increasingly polarized along partisan lines and it is not always easy to know what could become politically feasible.

The fundamental goal of the policy options we consider is to better protect the well-being of low-income Americans by reducing their vulnerability to the hardships of economic downturns and slow recoveries, as the U.S. has recently experienced with the Great Recession. Before describing our near-term policy reforms and long-term suggestions for better managing hardship in future economic downturns and recoveries, we discuss the difficulties faced by both Republicans and Democrats in reaching some sort of consensus. We argue that continued political stalemate presents real risks to America's most vulnerable citizens. We hope that our recommendations will help the leadership of the country move past this stalemate and better protect the well-being of low-income Americans.

The Difficult Paths: Liberal and Conservative Dreams

The near-term (2013–2020) challenge is to offer as much assistance to low-income Americans as possible during the slow recovery without exacerbating the federal government's long-term deficit, and without shifting spending burdens from the federal government to the state governments, since most states already face difficult or overwhelming fiscal challenges. We focus on what steps can be taken by the federal government, in part because the federal safety net is three times larger than the average state safety net[252] and in part because a careful analysis of each of the 50 states is beyond the scope of this book.

Liberal advocates of anti-poverty measures are quick to point to new revenues (or tax increases) as a promising path to bolstering America's safety net. A wide range of possibilities are suggested: repeal of the Bush-era tax cuts, at least for high-income Americans; closing of tax loopholes in the personal and corporate income tax codes; creation of a new value-added tax (VAT), as practiced in many European countries; and/or enactment of a new tax on greenhouse gases that can simultaneously reduce pollution and raise new revenues. We shall not address the complex economic and political issues associated with any of these proposals, except to say that any form of federal tax increase will very likely encounter determined opposition in the U.S. Congress, especially if the recovery remains slow. President Obama was unable to accomplish repeal of the Bush tax cuts for high-income Americans when the Democrats enjoyed a 60–40 margin in the United States Senate (2009–2010) and firm majority control of the House of Representatives.

It may also seem reasonable to look for additional resources for the safety net from savings at the Department of Defense, where fiscal year 2011 spending passed the $685 billion mark. Prominent leaders of both political parties have called for more restraint in defense spending but there is not much agreement about how any savings should be reallocated. The declining U.S. military commitments in Iraq and Afghanistan have freed up some resources, but defense specialists point out that many important security programs have been neglected during the past decade, in part due to the high priority given to the occupations of Iraq and Afghanistan. A careful assessment of military spending is beyond the scope of our inquiry.

Conservatives will be quick to propose reductions in domestic federal spending on both philosophical and deficit-reduction grounds.[253] It is useful therefore to remember where the big money is and which programs imperil the federal government's long-term fiscal future.

In fiscal year 2011, Social Security and Medicare cost the federal government $725 billion and $447 billion, respectively. These are not fully means-tested programs, though both programs have evolved in subtle ways to incorporate a degree of means-testing.[254] They are entitlement programs that benefit tens of millions of middle-class and wealthy Americans as well as low-income Americans.

In fiscal year 2011, more than twice as much federal money was expended on these two programs than the sum of federal spending on Medicaid, SNAP, Unemployment Insurance, TANF, and federal housing assistance.

Some have argued that some means-testing (involving income or assets) be added to eligibility for Social Security and Medicare, and/or that the age of eligibility for benefits be raised.[255] Liberals counter that if Social Security and Medicare become means-tested, they will become vulnerable to excessive cuts, since participation will not be universal in the electorate.[256]

While some conservatives advocate means-testing of all entitlement programs, rank-and-file Republicans in the Congress may refrain from voting in favor of entitlement reform (without bipartisan support) because they believe that Democrats will use those cuts as ammunition prior to the next election. Unless the Democrats in Congress are willing to join Republicans in a bipartisan effort at reducing spending growth in Social Security and Medicare, conservative initiatives to streamline Medicare and Social Security will not make much headway among re-election-minded Republican members of Congress. And Democrats have little incentive to discuss reform of Medicare and Social Security until new tax revenues are accepted as part of the grand solution.

As a practical matter, the Republican and Democratic parties appear to have taken off the table the two fiscal strategies that could have the most long-run, deficit-reducing promise: higher taxes and less spending on Medicare and Social Security. Some analysts see a possible "grand bargain" emerging in 2013–14, a long-term deal to reduce the federal deficit through entitlement reform and tax increases.[257] In the event such a deal is not found in the near-term, which we think is the likely scenario, the prospects for the federal government's continued level of support of the safety net are not good.

How a Fiscal Stalemate Puts the Poor at Risk

The federal government is now recording annual budget deficits that are the largest as a share of the economy since the end of World War II. As a result, the amount of federal debt held by the public is mushrooming.

From the end of 2008 to the end of 2012, the total federal debt as a percent of the nation's economy rose from 40% to 70%. Under plausible assumptions (equivalent to no "grand fiscal bargain"), the amount of debt held by the public could exceed 100 percent of Gross Domestic Product by 2021. Debt as a share of GDP may exceed its historical peak of 109 percent by 2023 and could reach 190 percent by 2035.[258]

If the "grand bargain" does not occur, Congress is almost forcing itself to put the safety net on the table because (a) it is the only remaining part of the federal budget that is large (excluding defense),[259] and (b) the political pressures for action against the annual federal deficit are intensifying.[260] Since the safety net was used by many during the worst downturn since the Great Depression, it has reached a spending peak and thus is a target for fiscal hawks looking for savings.

Ron Haskins of the Brookings Institution estimates that the ten largest means-tested federal programs accounted for $626 billion in federal spending in fiscal year 2011. Spending hawks will point to the fact that this figure is much larger than the $126 billion spent in 1980. (These figures are in dollars of the same purchasing power, so the effect of inflation is removed.) Much of this growth has occurred in the aftermath of the Great Recession, from $426 billion to $626 billion, when the Obama administration and Congress took special pains to protect low-income Americans. While much of the growth since 1980 has been in health care expenditures (Medicaid and CHIP), spending for SNAP, SSI, housing assistance, and EITC has also grown rapidly since 1980 and in recent years.[261]

Given this history, the case will be made that the safety net must be cut because the United States cannot afford it and the other sources of possible savings are off the table (Medicare, Social Security, and Defense). In reality, with one big programmatic exception (Medicaid), spending on the means-tested safety net is projected to decline from now until 2022—assuming a slow yet full recovery—both as a percent of GDP and in absolute terms. The rapid decline in spending on Unemployment Insurance alone will be sufficient to cover the few areas of safety-net spending that are projected to rise.[262] Thus, the single most important fact that low-income Americans (and their supporters) need entered into fiscal deliberations is that the federal safety net—except for Medicaid—is not a significant contributor to the country's long-term fiscal crisis.

Assisting Low-Income Families During the Recovery

Indexation of the Federal Minimum Wage

As the economy recovers, more low-income Americans are finding work, but a full-time job does not eliminate the risk of poverty. Before the onset of the Great Recession, about two million individuals in the United States were living in poverty each year, even though someone in the household worked full-time and year-round.[263]

In 2010 about 72.9 million workers in the United States were paid by the hour, and about 1.8 million earned exactly the prevailing federal minimum wage of $7.25 per hour. Another 2.5 million were paid less than the minimum wage, due to a variety of exemptions to the minimum wage. Workers who toil at (or below) the minimum wage fall disproportionately into at least one of the following categories: women, under the age of 25, no high school diploma, and living in the South. Some salaried employees may also be paid, in effect, less than the minimum wage, but the federal government does not collect detailed data on employees at the low end of the salary scale.[264]

Part of the low-wage employee problem is structural. As we discussed in Chapter 3, the "post-industrial" U.S. economy has fewer high-paying manufacturing jobs and more low-paying service jobs. Although the service sector is quite diverse, the fastest growing component of the service sector is "trade and personal services," which is dominated by low-wage positions in retail, wholesale, entertainment, and recreational industries. People working in this sector often have wages concentrated near the minimum wage, and they do not necessarily escape poverty through employment.

But the recovery from the Great Recession is already posing a new difficulty for the working poor: inflation. Prior to the recession (2003–07), the yearly rate of inflation in the U.S. economy (computed based on the Bureau of Labor Statistics Consumer Price Index) was averaging between 2 and 4 percent. The forces of the Great Recession ultimately did a favor for consumers: the elimination of inflation and in fact a modest amount of deflation from December 2008 to October 2009. The average annual rates of inflation for 2009 and 2010 were -0.4 percent and +1.6 percent, respectively. In 2010 and 2011, however, the rate of inflation appears to have returned to its pre-Recession levels, as it averaged 3.2 percent in 2011 and a bit less than 3 percent in the early months of 2012.[265]

The federal minimum wage is not adjusted automatically for the rate of inflation in the prices of goods and services. After the longest period in American history when the federal minimum wage was not raised, Congress did raise the minimum from $5.85 per hour in July 2007 to $7.25 per hour in July 2009. However, although Barack Obama campaigned in 2008 on a platform to index the federal minimum wage to the rate of inflation, Congress has not yet enacted an automatic indexation provision similar to what is already present in several state minimum wage laws.

For workers who are paid at the rate specified by the federal minimum wage, the absence of indexation means that the real purchasing power of their $7.25 per hour wage is already being eroded during the economic recovery. If the rate of inflation hovers around 3 percent from 2011 through 2015, the real (inflation-adjusted) worker wage in 2015 will have declined to $6.23 per hour. Unless a multi-person household has multiple workers, a real wage of $7.25 per hour is unlikely to be large enough to enable the household to escape poverty.

Critics of the federal minimum wage argue that the presence of the minimum wage raises the cost of labor to employers and causes fewer jobs to be made available to unskilled laborers. There is a large body of economic research on this question that does not come to a definitive conclusion.[266] While some workers probably do lose their current positions when the minimum wage is raised and some low-wage positions are never created, the total amount of wages received among low-skilled workers may ultimately rise since the larger number of workers who retain their positions benefit from higher wages. Moreover, there is some evidence that higher wages at the bottom of the wage scale improves worker productivity, so the consequences for firms are not entirely negative.

Despite our agreement on this policy proposal, we note that many conservative Republicans are likely to oppose any increase in the federal minimum wage (including an indexation policy). However, it may be feasible to attract limited Republican support in Congress in conjunction with near-unanimous support from congressional Democrats. As we were discussing this proposal, one of us (Graham) noted that President George W. Bush supported the most recent hike of the federal minimum wage (in part through a deal with a Democratic-controlled Congress that included more tax relief for small businesses), and Mitt Romney's campaign for president in 2012 received some (rare) positive remarks from liberal publications due to his stance in favor of automatic adjustment of the federal minimum wage based on the cost of living.[267]

Indexation of the minimum wage will help only a small fraction of families living below or near the poverty line. It will not help families escape poverty if no one is working or if the number of hours worked is too small. Many workers in impoverished families already have wages above the federal minimum. Over 80 percent of the earnings changes generated by increases in the minimum wage will accrue to non-poor families. Thus, raising the federal minimum wage, though it will help some poor families, is too blunt an instrument to have a large poverty-reducing impact.[268]

Finding Efficiencies within the Safety Net

Due to the long duration of the recovery (2009–2020), many families will continue to need support from federal safety net programs. However, the public demand for fiscal austerity will create pressure on politicians to reduce federal spending on the safety net. Even the more liberal of the two of us (Seefeldt) admits that efforts to enhance the efficiency of the safety net may be necessary to maintain political support for the safety net.

Since it seems inevitable that Congress will look for savings in the $641 billion federal safety net, it is crucial that the search for efficiencies be constructive rather than destructive. We suggest three near-term options: Medicaid reform, improved targeting of federal transfer programs, and reallocation of federal funds from non-poverty to anti-poverty programs.

Medicaid Reform. If one begins to look for efficiencies within the federal safety net, the Medicaid program must be the highest priority. It is by far the largest federal anti-poverty program and Medicaid spending has grown rapidly—during recoveries as well as recessions—since its inception in the 1960s. From an auditing perspective,

Medicaid is also considered a high-risk program because of the extent of program mismanagement that has been documented in the past.

Many states see a slowdown in the growth of Medicaid spending as their only viable path to fiscal sustainability. Even more growth in Medicaid spending is expected since the U.S. Supreme Court upheld the Affordable Care Act. A large expansion of Medicaid eligibility starts in 2014. The Act also compels states to reimburse providers under Medicaid at the higher rates now used by the Medicare program. The 2014 requirements are accompanied by substantial new federal funds, but those funds decline to some extent by 2020. Thus, any serious effort to restrain federal spending on the safety net must give priority to Medicaid but the fiscal problems of the states cannot be exacerbated.

"Medicaid reform" is defined here as measures to reduce Medicaid spending, without reducing patient access to care or the quality of services and without shifting fiscal burdens between levels of government. If successful Medicaid reform can be implemented, the ultimate result will be less fiscal pressure on both federal and state governments. Without Medicaid reform, elected officials may ultimately feel compelled to pare back Medicaid benefits, reduce eligibility and access to care, or cut funding for non-health anti-poverty programs (e.g., SNAP).

Both of us believe that the solution lies in changing the delivery of care for Medicaid patients without compromising access or quality or unduly raising the cost burden on the patient. A variety of states are seeking to reform treatment of Medicaid patients in ways that will reduce cost while maintaining (or even improving) quality of care.

One strategy that many states are pursuing is greater use of primary care physicians at offices and clinics (instead of emergency rooms) to deliver treatment for hundreds of diagnoses such as common infections, mild burns, strains, and bruises.[269] The hospital emergency room is not well designed to provide cost-effective care for non-urgent conditions, even though some Medicaid patients have turned to emergency rooms as their principal source of care.

The State of Washington, for example, has put pressure on the management of hospitals. Starting in 2012, if a Medicaid enrollee comes to an emergency room and is diagnosed with one of about 500 common conditions, the Washington Medicaid program will not reimburse the hospital or doctor for treatment. Moreover, services such as pregnancy tests, well-baby exams, and narcotics treatment are not best provided in an emergency room. Instead, the state will pay a screening fee of $50 to the hospital if the patient is in a private-plan version of Medicaid, the type of plan that currently enrolls 60 percent of patients in Washington and is expected to grow further in the future. The state expects emergency room personnel to make a quick assessment and steer patients to a cost-effective venue for care, such as an urgent-care clinic, a substance-abuse clinic, or a physician's office.

Tennessee adopted a similar plan for all "non-urgent" diagnoses unless the patient is under the age of two, in which case treatment in the emergency room will be reimbursed. Iowa, on the other hand, reduces (but does not eliminate) payments for non-urgent conditions and does not apply the policy to patients under the age of 21.

Medicaid reforms that seek to rationalize emergency room care should be carefully evaluated, since many hospital leaders and medical personnel are skeptical of how well these reforms will work in practice. Some patients who are not sure whether their condition is urgent may be dissuaded from seeking the care they need. Moreover, hospitals and their personnel may have ethical or liability reasons for offering care for some non-urgent conditions (e.g., urinary-tract infections), yet no reimbursements will occur under Medicaid. Instead of targeting all Medicaid patients, some hospitals argue that the focus should be on a small fraction of Medicaid patients who make extensive and inappropriate use of emergency rooms. The reforms may work better in a setting where Medicaid reimbursement rates are set equal to the higher Medicare rates, since physicians outside the emergency room will not be discouraged financially from treating Medicaid patients.

A second and complementary strategy is transitioning Medicaid patients from fee-for-service arrangements to managed care. In theory, greater reliance on managed care could improve patient health status while reducing overall health care expenditures.

Under fee for service, a physician (or other provider) is reimbursed for the delivery of care on a service-by-service basis. Concerns have been raised that this arrangement does not encourage providers to keep their patients healthy (e.g., by offering preventive services) and may lead to more costly patterns of care than is medically necessary. An advantage of fee for service is that a patient may seek care from any physician that takes Medicaid patients.

Under managed care, a network of providers (often a private health care company that specializes in Medicaid patients) is paid a fixed monthly payment for each Medicaid patient enrolled in the network's plan. The network includes primary care physicians as well as specialists. Each enrollee has a primary care physician, who is responsible for making referrals to specialists as appropriate. However, the enrolled patient must use the physicians in the network, and thus there is less choice than exists under fee for service.

The financial risk under managed care is typically shouldered by the networks, since they must provide patients the basic services covered by their plan, even if the costs of those services should prove to be greater than Medicaid's fixed payment for that patient. Under this financial arrangement, states can predict their fiscal obligations under Medicaid and networks have incentives to take creative steps that will keep their patients healthy.

About two-thirds of Medicaid enrollees are already covered, at least for some services, by managed care. States are rapidly expanding their use of managed care, in part to gain some control over the explosive growth of spending under the program.[270] Historically, managed care arrangements were targeted at women, children, and young adults, but some states are making efforts to shift the disabled and elderly to managed care.

Empirical studies show that managed care does work (i.e., does improve health and reduce spending) in some cases, but not all managed care arrangements have been effective.[271] While this form of Medicaid reform is promising and should be encouraged, it is not a panacea. Indeed, there are well-documented horror stories of low-income patients who could not obtain the prompt care they needed through a managed care arrangement.[272] Rigorous evaluation mechanisms need to be put in place by networks, states, and the federal government to ensure that the promise of managed care is realized.

Improved Targeting of Transfer Programs. When government transfers money from some citizens to others, one might expect low-income Americans to be the primary beneficiary of the transfer.

Recent studies call into question this expectation. For example, if we define low-income Americans as those at the bottom 20 percent of the U.S. income distribution, the best estimates are that this group received 54 percent of transfer dollars in 1979 but only 36 percent in 2007, prior to the onset of the Great Recession.[273]

To a large extent, the shift in the share of transfer payments away from low-income families is accounted for by the rapid growth of Medicare and Social Security. Expenditures under both programs have grown due to demographic changes—a significant increase in the proportion of the population who are elderly, coupled with increased life expectancy. And Medicare spending has been fueled by technological advances in medicine and other factors. Since Social Security and Medicare are not means-tested (i.e., like SNAP or Medicaid), those who pay Social Security taxes during their working years are entitled to collect a benefit, regardless of their prior earnings and wealth holdings.

Perhaps some better targeting of these two programs is needed. An analysis of IRS records for 2009 found that individuals in the top 1 percent of the income distribution claimed approximately $7 billion in Social Security benefits, or an average check of $33,000 for those with incomes exceeding $10 million.[274] Even in its current form, though, about 75 percent of Social Security benefits go to individuals with non-Social Security incomes of less than $20,000 per year. More than 90 percent of the benefits go to individuals with non-Social Security incomes of less than $50,000 per year. In order to avoid perverse incentives (e.g., strong disincentives to work), any decline in the Social Security benefits for higher-income individuals must decline gradually as income rises. Thus, the extent of fiscal savings from means-testing of Social Security is not huge.[275]

Consider also the difference between Medicare and Medicaid, and how much their benefits are targeted at households in the bottom 20 percent of the income distribution. In 2007 about 46.1 percent of Medicare benefits were received at the bottom quintile of the income distribution compared to 64.6 percent of Medicaid benefits.[276] In other words, a dollar spent on Medicaid is much more likely to benefit a low-income household than a dollar spent on Medicare. Since some elderly Americans have substantial assets but low incomes, the income-based data may exaggerate the extent to which Medicare helps households that lack the means to pay for care (or for insurance) with their own resources.

Both of us agree that the political feasibility of greater means-testing of Medicare or Social Security is doubtful.[277] Both programs are popular in part because they are not fully means-tested and in part because they benefit primarily a large, politically active subpopulation: the elderly. Moreover, the design of the programs fosters a rhetorical claim that everyone can count on Medicare and Social Security sooner or later, even though the financial foundations of such a commitment may not be solid. If Social Security and Medicare were fully means-tested, they might be too easy for politicians to cut (since the beneficiary population would be reduced dramatically). The social insurance programs of Western Europe, though they have contributed some to fiscal distress, have been durable in part because all citizens realize they can access them when they need to.

The argument that American citizens and their politicians will not support large investments in means-tested programs is not entirely consistent with the historical evidence.[278] The Medicaid program has grown steadily and dramatically since its inception in the 1960s. SNAP has also grown explosively. And the growth rates of SSI and federal housing assistance since 1980 have been large. On the other hand, the size of TANF's basic block grant for non-disabled adults—the only form of cash assistance for many low-income families—has been unchanged since 1996, when Congress eliminated such cash assistance as a federal entitlement.

After many rounds of disagreement, we both concluded that there are some modest forms of means-testing that would slow the rate of spending on Social Security and Medicare without a radical change in the politics of the programs. For example, the rate of growth of Social Security benefits for households with large incomes and/or assets could be moderated, or benefits could start at an older age, as suggested by the debt-reduction commission appointed by President Obama. Likewise, Congress could consider making Social Security and Medicare more like the Earned-Income Tax Credit: a strong focus on the low-income population but also significant benefits for families between the 20th and 40th (and even 60th) percentile of the income distribution. If Social Security were to be modified in this way, it would be somewhat less expensive for the federal government but the program would still have a large and diverse political constituency.

Even if Social Security and Medicare cannot (or should not) be means-tested, the data also suggest that Medicaid could be better targeted. In 2007 an estimated 12.9 percent of Medicaid benefits were received by households that were not in the bottom 40 percent of the nation's income distribution.[279] To be fair, a household of three at the bottom 40 percent of the income distribution might have an income of $30,000, which is hardly adequate when the high cost of private health insurance is considered. Moreover, some of these benefits to the non-poor may accrue to children under CHIP (which has more liberal income tests than Medicaid), and subjecting these children to the risks of private health insurance does not seem wise.[280] Nonetheless, even a small percentage of mis-targeting in a program the size of Medicaid presents a significant fiscal opportunity, an opportunity to redirect resources to families in urgent need of assistance. We recommend further studies be undertaken to determine how targeting in the Medicaid program might be improved to reduce the program's fiscal burden without harming genuinely needy households.

SNAP is a generally regarded as a well-targeted program,. About 85 percent of households receiving SNAP benefits have incomes (excluding SNAP assistance) below the federal poverty guideline. The average household receiving SNAP benefits had an income (excluding the value of SNAP benefits) of $8,800 per year. On average, SNAP benefits raised the average monthly income by 39 percent for all participating households and by 45 percent for households with children.[281] Thus, there is no question that SNAP is an important source of public assistance for many very poor households.

If SNAP can be criticized on grounds of targeting, it is because most states do not apply asset tests to the large numbers of SNAP recipients who are deemed "categorically eligible"—which means that they automatically qualify for SNAP because they receive (or are eligible to receive) other government benefits, including non-cash benefits under TANF. (Those non-cash benefits may be child care, transportation, or even a pamphlet or other information about TANF programs). If standard income and asset tests were applied to the automatically eligible recipients, the number of SNAP recipients might decline by 4 percent over the next ten years.

The savings in federal expenditures would be modest, about $1.2 billion per year, or less than 2 percent of projected federal spending on SNAP between 2013 and 2022.[282] We conclude, therefore, that if politicians are inclined to improve targeting in the federal safety net, more savings are likely to be found in Medicaid than in SNAP.

Budgetary Reallocations to Anti-Poverty Programs. Government expends taxpayer dollars—or offers tax credits—for a wide range of worthy purposes (e.g., education and environmental protection) where the policy is not designed specifically to benefit low-income Americans. We refer to these measures as "non-poverty" policies even though they may have some poverty-reducing impact. For example, government support for public schools in a mixed-income community will benefit some low-income as well as middle-income and upper-income households.

We suggest that some of these non-poverty policies could be redesigned to serve their worthy public purpose while also being targeted at low-income households. For example, a recent analysis of IRS data by Investor's Business Daily found that the top 1 percent of income-earners in 2009 reported the receipt of about $10 billion in transfer payments, such as Social Security benefits.[283] A much larger amount of revenue to the federal government was lost due to tax credits, deductions, and exemptions that households in the top 1 percent of the income distribution are authorized to take. Policy analysts should consider ways to redirect such payments and foregone revenue to programs that will benefit low-income Americans. We encourage policy makers to think broadly about the types of non-poverty policies that could be redesigned, as the following example illustrates.

Currently, the federal government promotes sales of electric cars through income tax credits and direct grants for recharging stations. We assume that there are good environmental and/or energy-security rationales for government policies that promote the electric car.

Specifically, purchasers of electric cars—whose average income is typically above $100,000 per year—are eligible for a $7,500 credit on their federal personal income tax. In 2009 alone, the top 1 percent of earners in the United States claimed about $31 million in tax credits related to their purchases of electric cars. The volume of those credits is expected to grow rapidly in the years ahead, as vehicle manufacturers offer more electric vehicles for sale. The Department of Energy has also allocated more than $170 million of federal "stimulus" monies for recharging stations in selected urban areas around the country. Several states are offering additional subsidies for recharging equipment in homes, offices, or community settings. Since few low-income Americans can afford an electric car, it is unlikely that these tax credits or infrastructure grants benefit motorists in the bottom of the income distribution.

Meanwhile, holding onto a job is crucial to reducing the need for public assistance, and access to a reliable car is crucial to obtaining—and holding onto—a productive job. Some states have used TANF dollars to support low-income car ownership. One such program is the non-profit Ways to Work, which has 55 offices in 23 states. This program offers auto loans (8 percent interest) to working families with bad credit scores who would otherwise not qualify for conventional loans. To qualify for a Ways to Work loan, recipients must satisfy an income eligibility test and take a financial literacy course. Since its beginning about a decade ago, Ways to Work has issued 32,000 loans worth $63 million.

A survey of 445 Ways to Work recipients by ICF International Inc. covered loans offered from 2007 to 2010 to low-income individuals. ICF found that 82 percent of the loan recipients were able to obtain better employment and reduce their dependence on public assistance programs. The estimated savings to the taxpayer were $18.2 million per year, much more than the $5.1 million in loans backed by private donations. In other words, about $2.50 in taxpayer money was saved for each dollar donated to the program for subsidized car loans.[284] Due to a lack of government support, Ways to Work relies on private donations to subsidize the auto loans.

Instead of providing tax credits and grants to wealthy individuals interested in electric cars, Congress might consider subsidizing the use of electric cars by low-income Americans. Although electric cars are $10,000 to $20,000 more expensive than gasoline cars of similar size, they offer several appealing features for low-income Americans: the price of electricity is 60–70 percent cheaper than gasoline, or about $1.50 per gallon when expressed on an energy-equivalent basis; and the driving range of electric vehicles (typically less than 100 miles on a single charge) is adequate to meet the commuting needs of most commuters living in urban areas.

The city of Paris, France, for example, has made a large fleet of electric cars available for community use, similar to the bike-sharing programs operating in many cities around the world. Residents can rent a vehicle for several hours or a day and then return it. This model could become an anti-poverty program if the low-income users of electric cars were shielded from the up-front cost of purchasing the vehicle through subsidized leasing arrangements or subsidized rates for each daily use of a vehicle. Although thought needs to be given to how such a program should be designed, implemented, and evaluated, it seems likely that the federal government's program to promote the use of electric cars could be redesigned in a way that would meet energy-security and environmental goals while also contributing to the war on poverty in urban communities.

More generally, it may be useful for policy makers to require that poverty-impact analyses be conducted for some or all non-poverty policies that are under consideration by legislators and regulators. Environmental impact analyses have certainly played an important role in bringing environmental considerations to the attention of policy makers in many different fields. If concerns about low-income Americans were raised more consistently in public debates about non-poverty policies, it seems more likely that creative options would be developed to serve the primary public purpose while also assisting (or at least not harming) low-income Americans.

Long-Term Reform for a Stronger Safety Net

TANF Reform

The Temporary Assistance to Needy Families (TANF) program is the only safety net program that provides cash to very low-income, non-disabled families, but it did not respond well to the hardships of the Great Recession. After falling to historic low levels in the late 1990s, TANF caseloads moved upward slightly during the 2001 recession, slowly declined after that, and then rose again very slightly at the onset of the Great Recession. Compared to the vast need for benefits among the very poor, the new poor, and the near poor, the TANF increase was rather paltry and not spread evenly throughout the country. The limited reach to families with children is particularly of concern. When welfare reform was enacted in 1996, TANF provided benefits to approximately 68 out of every 100 poor families with children; in 2010, TANF served only 27 out of every 100 poor families with children.[285] While some of the disabled children may be covered by SSI, the TANF program did not respond robustly to the Great Recession.

A number of the regulations and guidance documents governing TANF discourage states from increasing their caseloads, even during difficult economic times. States must meet a work participation rate of 50 percent, meaning that 50 percent of adult TANF recipients must be employed or participating in "work activities" for 30 hours a week (20 if the parent has a child under the age of six and 35–55 hours for two parent families). Initially, states had discretion to define what sorts of activities counted as work activities, and some states used this flexibility to place recipients in mental health programs or other rehabilitation activities that were thought to remove "barriers" to employment. Provisions in the Deficit Reduction Act (DRA) of 2005 took away much of this discretion. To count toward the work requirement, recipients must participate an average of 20 of the 30 hours in "core activities," which are narrowly defined as employment or other work-like or work-focused activities such as community service, on-the-job-training, or job search. The other 10 hours may be participation in non-core activities, but these are also more narrowly defined post–DRA.[286]

States can lower their minimum work participation rate through a provision called the "caseload reduction credit." Each year, the participation rate can be reduced by one percentage point for every percentage point reduction in the number receiving TANF since 2005. For example, a state in which the TANF caseload had been reduced by seven percentage points since 2005 would need to meet a work participation rate of 43 percent instead of 50 percent. Since the actual work participation rate (i.e., the proportion who are working or in work activities) has ranged between 31 and 35 percent, most states have met the federal requirement only through application of the caseload reduction credit.[287]

Failure to meet the work participation rate can result in financial penalties. Although in practice no state has been penalized, the threat of monetary penalties remains. At the same time, states are not eager to spend money on TANF. Thus, states may be discouraged from serving all but the most work-ready recipients and/or allowing their rolls to increase. Recipients who may not be able to participate in work activities, such as those with significant health problems, may need costly services before they are able to work, but the incentive for states to provide these services is low, given that the activities will not count as participation. Some states have placed such individuals in state-funded programs, but during downturns, funding for these programs may be in danger. Overall, the incentives embedded within the caseload-reduction scheme are quite clear: continue to keep caseloads low in order to benefit from the credit.

Even taking as a given that TANF will remain a work-focused program, there are a number of changes that could be made to improve its performance during future downturns. First, Congress could consider returning to the pre-DRA definitions of activities that count toward the work requirement so that states have more flexibility to place recipients into activities that meet their needs or take into account the availability (or lack thereof) of jobs. For example, mental health treatment may be exactly what some families need. Or, the DRA requirements could remain in place with a provision to suspend work requirements when the unemployment rate in a state goes above a certain level. Alternatively, Congress could consider alternative measures of performance in TANF. Rather than simply focusing on work participation, states could be rewarded for outcomes such as increasing employment and earnings, improving education levels, or even reducing poverty.[288]

Finally, the caseload reduction credit should be eliminated. The credit encourages states *not* to serve needy families, an outcome that is counter-intuitive, particularly during recessions. TANF receipt is already low, and thus this is not an arena where a strong push for fiscal austerity makes sense.

In general, we believe that the structure of the TANF program seems to have been designed for a booming economy rather than the Great Recession and its relatively jobless recovery. TANF needs to be modernized to reflect the realities of the business cycle. Moreover, as we note below, TANF might be better seen as part of our nation's fiscal stabilization instruments, like UI or SNAP, which would also make it far more responsive to the needs of the poor during downturns and slow recoveries.

Unemployment Insurance Reform

Unlike TANF, the number of recipients of Unemployment Insurance benefits grew rapidly in response to the Great Recession. Nonetheless, changes could be made to broaden the reach of the program and thereby reflect the realities of today's labor market. The average duration of tenure in a job is declining, women are working outside the home, and low-paying service sector jobs are proliferating. UI is not well designed to reflect these realities.

UI is not intended to provide replacement of wages to those who quit jobs or are fired due to reasons of their own making (e.g., purposefully not following workplace rules), but there are circumstances under which a worker might quit a job or be fired that are not so clear-cut. Most states have rules in place (or interpretations of rules) that define acceptable reasons for quitting (or being fired from) a job and still being eligible for benefits. These include leaving due to incidents of domestic violence or sexual or other harassment on the job; becoming ill; or caring for an ill family member.[289] We suggest that each state make sure that such provisions for "acceptable quitting" are available.

Some states also deny UI benefits to part-time workers who lose jobs and will not take a full-time job. Women are disproportionately likely to leave jobs because of these events or to need part-time rather than full-time work. And women—probably more so than men—may be caring for ill parents or children, which makes full-time employment impractical. We suggest that states reconsider such restrictions.

UI also has a number of monetary requirements that potential beneficiaries must meet. All states require that applicants have a certain level of earnings over a "base period." In nearly all states, the base period is the first four out of the last five most recent calendar quarters prior to job loss. In other words, the most recent quarter of earnings is not counted in calculating qualifying earnings. Prior to widespread computerization, employment and earnings data were not available in a timely fashion, and UI systems did not have the most recent quarter of earnings available to them when determining eligibility. With today's technology, this requirement seems outdated. Additionally, low-wage workers are likely to be negatively affected by this requirement, since they may not meet the earnings requirement unless their most recent wages are counted.[290]

These and other defects in UI were recognized by a blue-ribbon advisory committee convened by President Bill Clinton, with some bipartisan support.[291] Subsequently, many states made changes to their UI systems, adopting alternative base periods (e.g., using earnings from the last four of four quarters) and broadening their definitions of "good cause." However, not all states have done so, and the application of these changes is not uniform across states. Under the 2009 Recovery Act, states were provided with monetary incentives to make these and other changes to modernize their UI systems, and 39 states made at least some changes. Those funds are no longer available, though. Congress could re-authorize the funding, perhaps requiring all states to at least make changes to the base period if they have not already done so and make other changes that would broaden eligibility for UI among jobless individuals.

All of these changes tend to increase state and federal spending on UI when it is needed. Since UI is designed to be highly responsive to the business cycle, it acts, as we note below, as a fiscal stabilization measure. Some extra spending on UI in a downturn is not a long-term threat to the fiscal health of the nation.

Subsidized Employment and Job Training

Despite the availability of TANF and UI, some individuals will not qualify, or will exhaust their UI benefits, or will hit the time limit in the TANF program. Nor does it make sense for young adults who are unemployed or underemployed but need job experience to be supported primarily through UI or TANF. In order to help these individuals, particularly in future downturns, federal funding could be made available for states to develop subsidized employment opportunities, as occurred when TANF Emergency Funds were released, or offer job training so that individuals have the skills to obtain in-demand jobs.

Subsidized employment programs use public dollars to help pay the wages of hires. The Works Progress Administration (WPA) put into place during the Great Depression is an example of a subsidized employment program, but today's programs tend to be much smaller in scale and target employment in the private or non-profit sector rather than in large, federally funded projects. In some regards, the various programs organized under AmeriCorps can be considered subsidized employment. Public and nonprofit organizations can apply for federal grants to subsidize the cost of hiring and training short-term employees to help them meet community needs in a variety of areas (e.g., education and environmental issues). While AmeriCorps members are considered volunteers, they are paid a living stipend.

Subsidized employment and training is likely to be attractive to some Republicans as well as Democrats for a variety of reasons. First, a subsidized employment program, if well-designed, creates jobs that would not otherwise have existed. Second, and in line with the importance Americans place on work, it provides support in the form of wages, rather than a government check with limited strings attached. And third, it helps recipients maintain ties to the labor market, which could subsequently help them obtain an unsubsidized position later on (e.g., when economic conditions improve).

When TANF Emergency Funds were available, 39 states employed nearly 260,000 low-income individuals in subsidized jobs. These efforts could be replicated during future downturns by requiring that Congress set aside funding when the unemployment rate rises above some level for a certain number of months. The funds should not be restricted to TANF recipients but made available for any individuals who have run out of UI benefits or otherwise experienced long-term unemployment. It is critical that young adults be a focus of at least some of these funds.

Another option to assist individuals whose benefits expire (or who are not eligible) and who face difficulty finding unsubsidized employment is placement in a job training program. We define "job training" here to mean a relatively short-term certificate program, likely offered by a community college that prepares individuals for jobs in high-demand areas. Students in these programs might train to become medical lab technicians or computer support specialists, or other jobs expected to have growth over the coming years. According to a survey conducted by the U.S. Government Accountability Office, most states provide information about other services, including job training programs, but currently there is not a requirement that states do so in any systematic effort.[292]

In his 2012 State of the Union address, President Obama announced his intention to create such a program for the long-term unemployed that is more streamlined and easy to access. Currently, job training in the U.S. is very fragmented, with limited funding coming from numerous sources and the level of services varying depending upon one's status. For example, workers who lost jobs because of trade-related reasons may be eligible for significant funding for job training through the Trade Adjustment Assistance (TAA) program, while other unemployed workers (e.g., recent high school or college graduates) with no special status may be provided assistance on a first come, first served basis.[293]

Skeptics argue that federal job training programs have a long history of ineffectiveness and thus should be defunded, not maintained or expanded.[294] There is merit in some skepticism. Academic studies of job training programs have found current training models to be less than ideal.[295] Yet there are numerous examples of high-quality training programs that have been evaluated and found effective at placing individuals into jobs. In general, these programs are characterized by close ties to local community colleges and partnerships with local industries and employers. We recommend that funds be made available to test out further iterations of these initiatives and, depending upon evaluation results, expanding those that show promise.[296]

Even programs such as AmeriCorps, which have uneven track records in formal evaluation studies, are recognized as serving a highly constructive purpose in the midst of a severe downturn and slow recovery. They keep young people connected to the labor market, learning how to be a professional and how to acquire a sense of attachment to community. When the unemployment rate for young adults is 10 to 20 percent or more, as it has been in most regions of the U.S. for the last several years, service in AmeriCorps or related programs seems much better than the bleak alternatives.

Make the Safety Net an Automatic Stabilizer. From the onset of the Great Recession, federal spending for the six major anti-poverty programs did not increase uniformly, Table 5 portrays the cumulative percentage growth in each program from fiscal year 2007 to 2011.

The rapid growth of unemployment compensation is directly tied to the large run-up in the unemployment rate, the long bouts of joblessness, and the extensions in benefits that have been authorized by Congress due to the slow recovery. The explanation for the large growth rate in food and nutrition spending is similarly related to the growth in unemployment and poverty, plus there has been a significant increase in the participation rate among eligible Americans. In other words, of Americans who are eligible for SNAP assistance, the fraction who take the benefit has climbed significantly during (and after) the Great Recession. Forecasts call for spending on unemployment compensation and federal food assistance to decline significantly by 2020—assuming the economy recovers.[297] Housing assistance has experienced the smallest percentage rise, presumably because it is not an entitlement program and is constrained by yearly appropriations limitations. The basic block grant for TANF has not grown since it was created in 1996, although a short-term TANF Emergency Fund was created as part of the 2009 Recovery Act. It provided temporary relief to states for the additional TANF costs induced by the Great Recession, but states are now dependent on the block grant again.

Table 5. Federal Spending (billions of $) on Programs to Assist Low-Income Americans in the United States: The Six Largest Programs.

Program	FY 2007	FY 2011	% Change
Medicaid	190.6	275.0	+44
Unemployment Compensation	32.5	117.2	+361
Food and Nutrition Assistance	48.7	95.7	+97
Supplemental Security Income	32.8	49.6	+51
Earned Income Tax Credit	38.3	55.7	+45
Housing Assistance	39.4	47.7	+21

Source: U.S. Office of Management and Budget, Budget of the U.S. Government, Fiscal Year 2013, Historical Tables 8.5 and 8.7.

The safety net might be improved if all of its major components responded automatically to the forces of the business cycle. Economists call such instruments "automatic stabilizers" because they stimulate the economy during a downturn (and early in a recovery) and they have a cooling effect as the economy nears full employment. That stabilizing influence occurs automatically, without the need for any debates and votes by politicians on the floor of Congress.

Compared to other discretionary forms of government stimulus (e.g., business tax cuts and subsidies for energy development), anti-poverty programs are more effective at boosting near-term economic activity because low-income Americans are the most likely to spend (rather than save) the money. If a boost in aggregate demand is needed to soften a recession or accelerate recovery, putting more money in the hands of low-income Americans is one of the best stimulus strategies. We recognize that fiscal stabilization is an inexact science but a predictable system of automatic stabilization based on economic indicators seems more reassuring then one that depends on the whims of political coalitions in Congress.

Fiscal conservatives will raise the concern that converting all anti-poverty programs (e.g., TANF and housing assistance) into entitlements (like SNAP and Medicaid) will only exacerbate the nation's long-term fiscal situation. To some degree, this concern is valid. Spending on SNAP, for example, is highly countercyclical (rising in downturns and declining near the economy's peaks), but the level of SNAP spending does not always decline to its pre-recession level, even after the economy has reached full employment again.[298] Although the reasons for this pattern are not fully understood, it may be that once eligible recipients learn about a safety-net program through participation, they are more likely to use it in future cycles.

The more basic point, however, is that spending on non-health anti-poverty programs (especially SNAP and Unemployment Insurance) does decline substantially once a recovery is well under-way. The long-term fiscal problems faced by the federal government are more strongly linked to trends in health-related programs (Medicare and Medicaid) and Social Security, programs whose growth is spurred by demographic changes and technology.[299]

Anti-poverty programs grow rapidly in recessions, as automatic stabilizers should, but they are not much of a threat to the long-term fiscal health of the country.[300]

Instead of converting TANF or housing assistance into an entitlement, which may seem politically unrealistic, Congress could authorize automatic changes in the size of the block grant to the states for TANF and housing based on the condition of the economy. As the economy enters a downturn and unemployment rises, the federal block grants would grow; as the economy recovers and nears its next peak, the size of the block grants would diminish. The size of the block grants should also be adjusted to account for inflation, so that the amounts available are not eroded over the long haul by the declining purchasing power of the dollar.

If the entire safety net is converted from discretionary programs to entitlements (with appropriate income and asset restrictions and work requirements) or to automatically adjusted block grants, and allowed to act as automatic stabilizers, Congress might not need to enact such ambitious discretionary fiscal packages when a downturn occurs. For example, if TANF, housing assistance, and state public assistance programs had operated automatically as entitlements or adjustable block grants during (and soon after) the Great Recession, some of the $787 billion stimulus package may not have been necessary. Since at most a third of the $787 billion was targeted directly at low-income Americans, more reliance on entitlements or adjustable block grants and less reliance on discretionary spending is likely to do more good for both the poor and the economy as a whole.

A fiscal hawk might argue that, even if all safety-net programs were entitlements, then Congress would simply have added the $787 billion stimulus in 2009 to the enlarged expenditures on the entitlement-oriented safety net. Alternatively, the $787 billion would have been added to the enlarged block grants. As a result, the debt burden on the public would be even larger than it is today. If this is true, procedural solutions may be available to constrain the spending habits of elected officials.

One approach is a constitutional restraint on the ratio of discretionary spending to GDP or on the ratio of discretionary spending to dedicated revenues. The latter approach, if enacted at the federal level with appropriate exemptions for wars and emergencies, would place the President and Congress under some of the pressures that governors and state legislatures already face (except we urge that federal entitlement programs and adjustable block grants in the safety net operate outside of the more demanding procedural constraints). However, such an amendment is unlikely to pass the required support of two-thirds of states in the near future, and caution is warranted when placing the federal budget under the same constraints faced by states (e.g., the lack of flexibility could be disastrous in ways that are not currently foreseeable), even with exemptions for wars and other emergencies.[301]

Another, perhaps less risky approach is to place discretionary spending under tighter procedural controls ranging from supermajority voting requirements in both the House and Senate to some form of dedicated revenue requirement for all discretionary spending. The procedural controls have the effect of raising the political price of more discretionary spending, without precluding it when bipartisan majorities recognize that it is clearly necessary.

In summary, the long-run reform we suggest is a comprehensive set of safety-net programs that operate more like automatic stabilizers (i.e., like Unemployment Insurance and SNAP) and less according to year-to-year political discretion (i.e., like TANF and federal housing assistance). Liberals might prefer that this reform be accomplished by converting TANF and housing assistance into entitlement programs. Even if conservatives have their way (and SNAP and Medicaid are handled more like TANF), the block grants should be transformed into automatic stabilizers by linking their annual size to the condition of the economy. Some regional or state-by-state variation in the annual adjustments would certainly be sensible, since some recessions hit some regions of the country harder than others. In other words, the size of the federal block grant to a state for anti-poverty assistance would rise (fall) as the rate of unemployment in a state falls (rises).

Politically, the terms of a grand bargain between the two political parties might be a strengthened anti-poverty program with fewer discretionary components, coupled with procedural constraints that raise the hurdle for discretionary spending, higher than it is under current procedures. We won't bet the ranch that

Congress will embrace the bargain tomorrow, but we believe that both political parties, low-income Americans, and the nation as a whole—if not Congress as an institution—have something to gain from the new arrangement.

Notes

Chapter 1

1. National Bureau of Economic Research, http://www.nber.org/cycles.html.

2. National Bureau of Economic Research, http://www.nber.org/cycles.html.

3. Allan Sloan, "Recession Predictions, and Investment Decisions," December 11, 2007, http://www.washingtonpost.com/wp-dyn/content/article/2007/12/10/AR2007121001589.html.

4. Hilary W. Hoynes, Douglas L. Miller, and Jessamyn Schaller, "Who Suffers During Recessions?" *NBER Working Paper* No. 17951, March 2012, http://www.nber.org/papers/w17951.

5. Carlos Torres, "Deep Recessions in U.S. May Be the Norm, Say NBER Economists," http://www.bloomberg.com/news/2012–03–22/deep-recessions-in-u-s-may-be-the-norm-say-nber-economists.html.

6. Michael Hout, Asaf Levanon, and Erin Cumberworth, "Job Loss and Unemployment," in *The Great Recession* (David B. Grusky, Bruce Western, and Christopher Wimer, Eds.), Russell Sage Foundation, New York, 2011, 60–61; Rebecca Thiess, "The Great Recession's Long Tail: Third Anniversary Underscores Severity of Labor Market Woes," Economic Policy Institute, February 2, 2011, http://www.epi.org/publication/bp294/.

7. Dennis Jacobe, "Underemployment Hits 20% in Mid-March," March 19, 2010, http://www.gallup.com/poll/126821/underemployment-hits-20-mid-march.aspx.

8. Jenny Marlar, "U.S. Unadjusted Unemployment Unchanged in June," July 5, 2012, http://gallup.com/poll/155486/Unadjusted-Unemployment-Unchanged-June.aspx.

9. U.S. Bureau of Labor Statistics, http://data.bls.gov/pdq/SurveyOutputServlet, retrieved July 6, 2012.

10. The Pew Charitable Trusts, "A Year or More: The High Cost of Long-Term Unemployment, Addendum," Pew Fiscal Analysis Initiative, May 2012, 1.

11. U.S. Bureau of Labor Statistics, "Changes to Data Collected on Unemployment Duration," http://www.bls.gov/cps/duration.htm.

12. Adrienne L. Fernandes-Alcantara, "Youth and the Labor Force: Background and Trends," Congressional Research Service, 7–5700, May 10, 2012.

13. Ibid., Table 2, 7–8.

14. Thomas A. Mroz and Timothy H. Savage, "The Long-Term Effects of Youth Unemployment," *Journal of Human Resources* 41(2), Spring 2006, 259–293.

15. Heidi Shierholz and Kathryn Anne Edwards, "The Class of 2011: Young Workers Face a Dire Labor Market Without a Safety Net." Economic Policy Institute, *Briefing Paper* #306, April 20, 2011.

16. Pew Research Center, *Young, Underemployed and Optimistic: Coming of Age, Slowly, in a Tough Economy*, Washington, DC, February 9, 2012.

17. Heidi Shierholz and Kathryn Anne Edwards, "The Class of 2011: Young Workers Face a Dire Labor Market Without a Safety Net," Economic Policy Institute, *Briefing Paper* #306, April 20, 2011, 12.

18. Pew Research Center, *Young, Underemployed and Optimistic: Coming of Age, Slowly, in a Tough Economy.* Washington, DC, February 9, 2012, 7.

19. Naomi Spencer, "Poverty Soars among Young Families in the U.S.," September 22, 2011, http://www.wsws.org/articles/2011/sep2011/pove-s22.shtml.

20. Spencer Jakab, "Unemployment Line Longer than it Looks," *Wall Street Journal*, July 6, 2012, C1.

21. This ratio is commonly used by the OECD, a think tank in Paris, when it compares economies around the world.

22. Bureau of Labor Statistics, U.S. Department of Labor, 2011, http://data.bls.gov/timeseries/LNS12300000.

23. When the rate of unemployment dropped from 9.0 to 8.6 percent in November 2011, it was estimated that about half of the improvement was an artifact of people no longer being counted as in the labor force. Ben Casselman, and Josh Mitchell, "Jobless Rate Nears Three-Year Law," *Wall Street Journal*, December 3, 2011.

24. Alex Kowalski, "Payrolls in U.S. Rose 80,000 in June; Jobless Rate 8.2%," *Bloomberg*, July 6, 2012, http://www.bloomberg.com/news/2012–07–06/payrolls-in-u-s-rose-80-000-in-june-jobless-rate-at-8–2–.html.

25. See Suzy Khimm, "Economic Outlook for 2012 Even Worse Than We Thought," Washington Post, November 14, 2011, http://www.washingtonpost.com/blogs/ezra-klein/post/forecast-for-2012-economy-even-worse-than-we-thought; Kiplinger, Economic Outlook, November 22, 2011, http://www.kiplinger.com/businessresource_outlook/;

26. http://www.dailyfx.com/forex/market_alert/2012/06/20/Federal_ Reserves_June_Economic_ ..., retrieved 7/6/2012; also see Binyamin Appelbaum. Without Output Stumbling, Fed Takes a Modest Step. New York Times. June 20, 2012.

27. U.S. Congressional Budget Office, CBO's 2011 Long-Term Budget Outlook, Washington, DC, June 2011, 25.

28. Paul Davidson, "Consumer Pessimism Continues," *USA Today*, May 14, 2012, B1.

29. Ibid.

30. Damian Paletta, "CBO Sees Recession Risk in 2013," *Wall Street Journal*, May 23, 2012, http://online.wsj.com/article/SB100014240527023 04019404577420592727486770.html.

31. Catherine Hollander, "Economy: The More Things Change," *National Journal*, April 6, 2012, 39–41.

32. Carlos Torres, "Deep Recessions in U.S. May be the Norm, Say NBER Economists," *Bloomberg*, March 22, 2012, http://www.bloomberg. com/news/2012–03–12/deep-recessions-in-us-may-be-the-norm, retrieved May 17, 2012.

Chapter 2

33. United Nations, *The Millennium Development Goals Report*, New York, UN, 2010.

34. National Research Council, Measuring Poverty: A New Approach, National Academy Press, Washington, DC, 1995, 1, 35 (hereafter cited as "NAS, 1995").

35. Kenneth Couch and Maureen Pirog, "Poverty Measurement in the U.S., Europe, and Developing Countries," *Journal of Policy Analysis and Management*, 29(2), 2010, 217–226.

36. Bruce D. Meyer and James Sullivan, "Viewpoint: Further Results on Measuring the Well Being of the Poor Using Income and Consumption," *Canadian Journal of Economics*, 44(1), 2011, 52–87; Bruce D. Meyer and James Sullivan, "Measuring the Well Being of the Poor Using Income and Consumption," *Journal of Human Resources* 38:S, 2003, 1180–1220; David M. Cutler and Lawrence F. Katz, "Macroeconomic Performance and the Disadvantaged," *Brookings Papers on Economic Activity*, 2, 1991, 1–74.

37. Robert Rector and Rachel Sheffield, "Understanding Poverty in the United States: Surprising Facts about America's Poor," *Backgrounder* #2607, Heritage Foundation, Washington, DC, September 13, 2001, http://www.heritage.org/research/reports/2011/07/what-is-poverty.

38. Brian Nolan and Christopher Whelan, "Using Non-Monetary Deprivation Indicators to Analyze Poverty and Social Exclusion: Lessons from Europe?", *Journal of Policy Analysis and Management*, 29(2), 2010, 305–325.

39. NAS, 1995, 31.

40. Mollie Orshanksy, "Children of the Poor," *Social Security Bulletin*, 26(7), July 1963, 3–13; "Counting the Poor: Another Look at the Poverty Profile," *Social Security Bulletin*, 28(1), January 1965, 3–29; "Who's Who Among the Poor: A Demographic View of Poverty," *Social Security Bulletin*, 28(7), July 1965, 3–32.

41. NAS, 1995, 24–25.

42. Disability programs and tax credits, for example, do not make use of the poverty threshold, http://www.irp.wisc.edu/faqs/faq1.htm.

43. The food share has declined while the share devoted to housing and transportation has increased. Laura Castner and James Mabli, "Low-Income Household Spending Patterns and Measures of Poverty," Mathematica Policy Research Inc., 6408–600, April 2010, xiii-xiv.

44. This treatment of medical care has been sharply criticized. See, for example, John F. Cogan, "Dissent," NAS, 2005, 385–390. See also Gary Burtless and Sarah Siegel, "Medical Spending, Health Insurance, and Measurement of American Poverty," Institute for Research on Poverty, University of Wisconsin, *Discussion Paper* No. 1238–01, September, 2001.

45. The measure proposed by NAS is "quasi-relative in nature," NAS, 1995, 23.

46. Kathleen Short, *The Research Supplemental Poverty Measure: 2010*, Census Bureau, Washington, DC, P60–241, November 2011.

47. Technically, the SPM threshold is based on mean expenditures on food, clothing, shelter, and utilities for families between the 30th and 36th percentile. Then this mean is multiplied by 1.2 to account for other spending. See p. 18 of http://www.census.gov/hhes/povmeas/methodology/supplemental/research/Short_ResearchSPM2010.pdf.

48. Jason DeParle, Robert Gebeloff, and Sabrina Tavernise, "Bleak Portrait of Poverty Is Off the Mark, Experts Say," *New York Times*, November 3, 2011.

49. Timothy M. Smeeding, Jeffrey P. Thompson, Asaf Levanon, Esra Burak, "Poverty and Income Inequality in the Early Stages of the Great Recession," in The Great Recession (eds., David B. Grusky, Bruce Western, Christopher Wimer), Russell Sage Foundation, New York, 2011, 91.

50. See, for example, Emily Monea and Isabel Sawhill, "An Update to Simulating the Effect of the 'Great Recession' on Poverty," Brookings Institution, Washington, DC, 2010; Julia B. Isaacs, "Predicting Child Poverty Rates During the Great Recession," *First Focus Report*, Brookings Institution, Washington, DC, December 2010; Timothy Smeeding, Jeffrey P. Thompson, and Esra Burak, "Poverty and Income Inequality in the Early States of the Great Recession," in *The Great Recession* (David B. Grusky, Bruce Western, and Christopher Winer), Russell Sage Foundation, New York, 2011, 83, 99–100.

51. Ron Haskins, "Reflecting on SNAP: Purposes, Spending, and Potential Savings," Testimony, House Subcommittee on Nutrition and Horticulture, May 8, 2012, , footnote 21 (discussing the forecasting model of Richard Bavier), http://www.brookings.edu/research/testimony/2012/05/08-snap-haskins.

52. Richard Wolf, "Fewer Draw on Federal Support," *USA Today*, May 29, 2012, 1A.

53. U.S. Department of Agriculture, SNAP Monthly Data, June 29, 2012, http://www.fns.usda.gov/pd/34snapmonthly.htm.

54. Emily Monea and Isabel V. Sawhill, "An Update to Simulating the Effect of the 'Great Recession' on Poverty," Brookings Institution, Washington, DC, September 13, 2011, http://www.brookings.edu/reports/2011/0913_recession_poverty_monea_sawhill.aspx.

55. Carmen DeNavas-Walt, Bernadette D. Proctor, and Jessica C. Smith, U.S. Census Bureau, Current Population Reports, P60–239, *Income, Poverty, and Health Insurance Coverage in the United States: 2010*, U.S. Government Printing Office, Washington, DC, September 2011 and P60–243, *Income, Poverty, and Health Insurance Coverage in the United States: 2011*, U.S. Government Printing Office, Washington, DC, September 2012.

56. Kathleen Short, *The Research Supplemental Poverty Measure: 2010*, Census Bureau, Washington, DC, P60–241, November 2011.

57. Carmen DeNavas-Walt, Bernadette D. Proctor, and Jessica C. Smith, op cit.

58. Miriam Jordan, "For First Time, Largest Group of Poor Children in U.S. Are Latino, Report Finds," *Wall Street Journal*, September 29, 2011.

59. Kathleen Short, *The Research Supplemental Poverty Measure: 2010*, Census Bureau, Washington, DC, P60–241, November 2011.

60. Carmen DeNavas-Walt, Bernadette D. Proctor, and Jessica C. Smith, op cit.

61. Authors' tabulations of U.S. Census data.

62. U.S. Census Bureau: http://www.census.gov/hhes/povmeas/methodology/supplemental/research/Renwick2009RevisedTables.pdf.

63. Danilo Trisi, Arloc Sherman, and Matt Broaddus, "Poverty Rate Second-Highest in 45 Years; Record Numbers Lacked Health Insurance, Lived in Deep Poverty," Center on Budget and Policy Priorities, September 14, 2011.

64. Robert D. Plotnick. "The Alleviation of Poverty: How Far Have We Come?," *Oxford Handbook of the Economics of Poverty* (Philip N. Jefferson, Ed.), January 2011 (draft), in press, 6.

65. H. Luke Shaefer and Kathryn Edin, "Extreme Poverty in the United States, 1996–2011," *National Poverty Center Policy Brief*, 2012,

http://www.npc.umich.edu/publications/policy_briefs/brief28/policy-brief28.pdf.

66. Ibid.

67. Maria Cancian and Sheldon Danziger (Eds.), *Changing Poverty*, 2009, New York: Russell Sage Foundation.

68. Richard V. Burkhauser, Jeff Larrimore, and Kosali I. Simon. "A 'Second Opinion' on the Economic Health of the American Middle Class," *NBER Working Paper* 17164, June 2011, http://www.nber.org/papers/w17164.

69. See, for example, Nicholas Eberstadt, "The Mismeasure of Poverty," *Policy Review* 138, August 1, 2006, http://www.hoover.org/publications/policy-review/article/6172, retrieved May 5, 2012.

70. Bruce D. Meyer and James X. Sullivan, "The Material Well Being of the Poor and the Middle Class Since 1980," American Enterprise Institute for Public Policy Research, *AEI Working Paper* #2011–04, October 25, 2011.

71. Ron Haskins, "Combating Poverty: Understanding New Challenges for Families," testimony to U.S. Senate Committee on Finance, June 5, 2012, http://www.brookings.edu/research/testimony/2012/06/05-poverty-families-haskins/.

72. Sheila R. Zedlewski and Austin Nichols, "What Happens to Families' Income and Poverty After Unemployment?", Urban Institute, May 31, 2012, Brief 25, Table 5, p. 6.

73. Ron Haskins, Congressional testimony, op cit.

74. Martha R. Burt and Demetra S. Nightingale, *Repairing the U.S. Social Safety Net*, Urban Institute Press, Washington, DC, 2010, 46.

75. Nicholas Eberstadt, "The Mismeasure of Poverty," *Policy Review* 138, August 1, 2006, http://www.hoover.org/publications/policy-review/article/6172.

76. Signe-Mary McKerman and Caroline Ratcliffe, "Events that Trigger Poverty Entries and Exits, " *Social Science Quarterly* 86 (Supplement), 2005, 1146–1169.

77. Sheldon Danziger and Peter Gottschalk, *America Unequal*, New York, Russell Sage Foundation, 1995.

78. William Julius Wilson, "Why Both Social Structure and Culture Matter in a Holistic Study of Poverty," *Annals of the American Academy of Political and Social Science*, 2010, 629: 200–219

79. John R. Logan, Elisabeta Minca, and Sinem Adar, "The Geography of Inequality: Why Separate Means Unequal in American Public Schools," *Sociology of Education*, 2012, (3) 287–301.

80. William Julius Wilson, *The Truly Disadvantaged*, Chicago, University of Chicago Press, 1987.

81. See Oscar Lewis, *Five Families: Mexican Case Studies in the Culture of Poverty*, 1959 and *La Vida: A Puerto Rican Family in the Culture of Poverty*, 1968.

82. Lawrence Mead, *Beyond Entitlement*, New York, Basic Books, 1986.

83. Charles Murray, *Losing Ground*, New York, Basic Books, 1984.

84. Javob L. Vigdor, *From Immigrants to Americans: The Rise and Fall of Fitting In*, Rowman and Littlefield, New York, 2009.

85. For the case that the rising flow of immigration helps explain why the overall rate of poverty has not declined in the U.S. since 1980, see Robert D. Plotnick, "The Alleviation of Poverty: How Far Have We Come?", *Oxford Handbook of the Economics of Poverty* (Philip N. Jefferson, Ed.), draft, January 2011, 25–6.

86. Jacob L. Vigdor, "Immigration: What the U.S. Does Right," *Los Angeles Times*, June 6, 2011, http://articles.latimes.com/2011/jun/06/opinion/la-oe-vigdor-immigration-20110606.

87. Sarah Reckhow and Margaret Weir, *Building a Stronger Regional Safety Net: Philanthropy's Role*, Brookings, July 21; 2011; Scott Allard, "Tackling Today's Poverty with Yesterday's Philanthropy," *The New Republic*, August 1, 2011.

88. Steven Raphael and Eugene Smolensky, "Immigration and Poverty in the United States," *Focus* 26(2), Fall 2009, 27–31; Jeff Chapman and Jared Bernstein, "Immigration and Poverty: How Are They Linked?", *Monthly Labor Review*, April 2003, 10–15.

89. Authors' tabulations of U.S. Census data.

90. U.S. Department of Justice, 2006, *Prisoners in 2005*, Washington, DC, U.S. Department of Justice.

91. Jeremy Travis, *But They All Come Back*, Washington, DC, Urban Institute Press, 2005.

92. Thomas and Sawhill, using microsimulation analyses, dispute the notion that there is a shortage of marriageable men. See Adam Thomas and Isabel Sawhill, "Marriage as an Antipoverty Strategy," *Journal of Policy Analysis and Management*, 2002, 21 (4): 587–599.

93. Pew Research Center, "The New Demography of American Motherhood," http://pewresearch.org/pubs/1586/changing-demographic-characteristics-american-mothers, 2010.

94. Kathryn Edin and Maria Kefalas, *Promises I Can Keep*, Berkeley, CA, University of California Press, 2005.

95. Robert Moffitt, "The Effect of Welfare on Marriage and Fertility," in R. Moffitt (Eds.), *Welfare, the Family, and Reproductive Behavior*, Washington, DC, National Academy Press, 1998.

96. U.S. Census, http://www.census.gov/compendia/statab/2012/tables/12s0627.pdf.

97. Kathryn Edin and Maria Kefalas, op cit.

98. J. Iceland and K. J. Bauman, "Income Poverty and Material Hardship: What is the Association?", *Journal of Socio-Economics,* 2007, 36, 376–396.

99. Michael Marmot, "Social Determinants of Health Inequalities," *The Lancet,* March 2005, 365:1099–1104, 19.

100. Jeanne Brooks-Gunn and Greg Duncan, "The Effects of Poverty on Children," *The Future of Children,* 1997, 7: 55–71.

101. Greg Duncan, Kathleen Ziol-Guest, and Ariel Kalil, "Early-Childhood Poverty and Adult Attainment, Behavior, and Health," *Child Development,* 2010, 81 306–325.

102. Ibid.

103. Gordon Berlin, "Investing in Parents to Invest in Children," 2007, MDRC, http://www.mdrc.org/publications/456/presentation.html

Chapter 3

104. Emily Kaiser, "Asia Weaves Strands of Safety Net," *Reuters,* March 12, 2012, http://www.reuters.com/article/2012/03/12/us-asia-inequality-idUSBRE82B0GZ20120312.

105. Alexandra Briscoe. Poverty in Elizabethan England. February 17, 2011, http://www.bbc.co.uk/history/british/tudors/poverty_01.shtml; History on the Net.com. The Tudors—Elizabethan Poor Law 1601, http://www.historyonthenet.com/Tudors/poor_law.htm.

106. James Patterson, *America's Struggle Against Poverty in the Twentieth Century,* Cambridge, MA, Harvard University Press, 2000.

107. Katie L. Roeger, Amy Blackwood, and Sarah L. Pettijohn, "The Nonprofit Sector in Brief: Public Charities, Giving, and Volunteering, 2011," *The Nonprofit Almanac 2011,* National Center for Charitable Statistics, The Urban Institute, http://www.urban.org/UploadedPDF/412434-NonprofitAlmanacBrief2011.pdf.

108. Elizabeth Boris, Erwin De Leon, Katie Roeger, and Milena Nikolova, "Human Service Nonprofits and Government Collaboration: Findings from the 2010 National Survey of Nonprofit Government Contracting and Grants," The Urban Institute, 2010, http://www.urban.org/publications/412228.html.

109. Holly Hall, "Donations Barely Grew at All Last Year, 'Giving USA' Finds," *Chronicle of Philanthropy,* June 19, 2012, http://philanthropy.com/article/Donations-Barely-Grew-at-All/132367/.

110. This estimate is based on a Pew Foundation survey of 2,048 adults ages 18 and older conducted December 6 to 19, 2011. There were no differences in such support by gender or race. Catherine Rampell, "I Get By With

a Little Help from My Parents," *New York Times,* March 19, 2012, http://economix.blogs.nytimes.com/2012/03/19/i-get-by-with-a-little-help-from-my -parents/.

111. http://www.census.gov/hhes/www/cpstables/032011/pov/new28_001_01.htm.

112. Betsy Brill, "The More Philanthropy Changes, the More It Stays the Same," Forbes.com, January 27, 2011, http://www.forbes.com/2011/01/27/philanthropic-giving-in-2011-brill-intelligent-investing.html.

113. Center on Philanthropy, "Patterns of Household Giving by Income Group, 2005," prepared for Google, Indiana University, Summer 2007.

114. Sheryl Sandberg, "The Charity Gap," April 4, 2007, http://online.wsj.com/article/SB117565580732059314.html.

115. C. Clotfelter, "Tax-Induced Distortions in the Voluntary Sector," *Case Western Law Review* 39, 1988/89, 663–694.

116. Rob Reich, "A Failure of Philanthropy: American Charity Short-changes the Poor, and Public Policy is Partly to Blame," *Stanford Social Innovation Review,* Winter 2005, 28.

117. Scott Allard, Sandra Danziger, and Maria Wathen, "Receipt of Public Benefits and Private Support among Low-Income Households with Children after the Great Recession," *Policy Brief* #31, National Poverty Center, April 2012, http://www.npc.umich.edu/publications/policy_briefs/brief31/PolicyBrief31.pdf.

118. Stephanie Strom, "Donors Weigh the Ideals of Meaningful Giving," *New York Times,* November 1, 2011, http://www.nytimes.com/2011/11/02/giving/donors-weigh-the-most-worthy-ways-to-give. .

119. Rich, Andrew, *Think Tanks, Public Policy, and the Politics of Expertise,* Cambridge, UK, Cambridge University Press, 2005.

120. Center for American Progress, "Bloomberg Tackles Poverty Differently: With Venture Capital-Driven Philanthropy," December 19, 2006, http://www.americanprogress.org/issues/2006/12/nyc_poverty.html.

121. Kate Hoagland, "Center for Economic Opportunity Wins Harvard Innovations in American Government Award," Ash Center for Democratic Governance and Innovation, Kennedy School of Government, Harvard University, February 12, 2012.

122. Glenn Pasanen, "Despite Scant Results, Bloomberg's Anti-Poverty Project Goes National," *GothamGazette,* May 2011, http://old.gothamgazette.com/article/finance/20110518/8/3529.

123. Press Release, Office of the Mayor of New York City, February 12, 2012, PR-053–12, http://www.nyc.gov/portal/site/nycgov/menuitem.

124. James Ricco et al., "Toward Reduced Poverty Across Generations: Early Findings from New York City's Conditional Transfer Program," MRDC, March 2010.

125. Julie Bosman, "City Will Stop Paying the Poor for Good Behavior," *New York Times*, March 30, 2010, http://www.nytimes.com/2010/03/31/ nyregion/31cash.html.

126. Binyamin Appelbaum, "Family Net Worth Drops to Level of Early 90's, Fed Says," *New York Times*. June 11, 2012, A1.

127. Jesse Bricker, Brian Bucks, Arthur Kennickell, Traci Mach, and Kevin Moore, "Surveying the Aftermath of the Storm: Changes in Family Finances from 2007 to 2009," *Finance and Economics Discussion Series 2011–17*, Board of Governors of Federal Reserve System, March 2011, http://www.federalreserve.gov/pubs/feds/2011/201117/index.html.

128. Binyamin Appelbaum, op cit.

Chapter 4

129. The phrase "low-income" refers generally to people who are poor or near-poor, usually with incomes less than some multiple of the official poverty line (e.g., 185% or 300%).

130. Tax Policy Center, "The Tax Policy Briefing Book," 2012, Washington, DC, Brookings Institution/The Urban Institute, http://www.tax-policycenter.org/briefing-book/.

131. Yonatan Ben-Shalom, Robert Moffitt, and John Karl Scholz, "An Assessment of the Effectiveness of Anti-Poverty Programs in the United States," *Discussion Paper* No. 1392–11, Institute for Research on Poverty, University of Wisconsin, Revised, June 2011.

132. The White House, *Creating Pathways to Opportunity*, October 2011, 6.

133. Average household size is 2.2 persons. USDA Food and Nutrition Service, 2011, http://www.fns.usda.gov/pd/snapmain.htm.

134. OMB, Budget of the U.S. Government, FY 2012, Historical Tables, 11.3 (estimate).

135. Note that participation data are reported by USDA through 2011 while eligibility data are reported only through 2009, http://www.fns. usda.gov/ora/MENU/Published/snap/FILES/Participation/ Trends2002–09.pdf.

136. Joshua Leftin, Esa Eslami, and Mark Strayer, "in Supplemental Nutrition Assistance Program Participation Rates: Fiscal Year 2002 to Fiscal Year 2009," USDA Food and Nutrition Service, 2010, http://www. fns.usda.gov/ora/MENU/Published/snap/FILES/Participation/ Trends2002–09.pdf.

137. U.S. Department of Agriculture. http://www.fns.usda.gov/ora/ MENU/Published/snap/SNAPPartState.htm.

138. Ron Haskins, "Reflecting on SNAP: Purposes, Spending, and Potential Savings," Testimony, House Subcommittee on Nutrition and

Horticulture, May 8, 2012, http://www.brookings.edu/research/
testimony/2012/05/08-snap-haskins.

139. Robert Greenstein, Center on Budgetary and Policy Priorities, testimony on "Strengthening the Safety Net," House Budget Committee, April 17, 2012, 13.

140. Approximately 40 states have no asset tests for SNAP assistance. Jennifer Steinhauer, "Millionaires on Food Stamps and Jobless Pay? GOP Is On It," *New York Times*, December 13, 2011, A17.

141. http://theccpp.org/issues-food-stamp-reform.html, posted 11/30/2011.

142. Ron Haskins, House Testimony, May 8, 2012, op cit.

143. For a summary of a series of papers on the effectiveness of Food Stamps, see Diane Whitmore Schanzenbach, "Food Stamps Seen as Efficient, Can Improve Health," *IPR Research Notes*, 33(1), Fall 2011, 5; Janet Currie, "U.S. Food and Nutrition Programs," in *Means-Tested Transfer Programs in the United States* (Robert Moffitt, Ed.), University of Chicago Press, Chicago, IL, 2003, 199–290; Mary Kay Fox, William Hamilton, and Bing-Hwan Lin, "Effects of Food Assistance and Nutrition Programs on Nutrition and Health, Volume 3," *Literature Review*, USDA, 2004.

144. Soon after taking office in January 1981, President Reagan suggested that the Food Stamp program be replaced with a block grant to the states. Carleson Center for Public Policy, "Issue: Food Stamp Reform," retrieved November 30, 2011, http://theccpp.org/issues-food-stamp-reform.html. More recently, a prominent Republican congressman, Paul Ryan, proposed a similar idea. See Linda Feldman, "Paul Ryan Sends Shockwaves through D.C. with New GOP Budget," *Christian Science Monitor*, April 5, 2011.

145. Center on Budget and Policy Priorities, http://www.cbpp.org/cms/index.cfm?fa=view&id=3534.

146. Ron Nixon, "Stack of Farm Proposals is Coming Up for Votes," *New York Times*, June 19, 2012.

147. Dorothy Rosenbaum and Stacy Dean, "Lucas-Peterson Proposal Would Throw 2–3 Million People off of SNAP," July, 2012, Center on Budget and Policy Priorities, http://www.cbpp.org/cms/index.cfm?fa=view&id=3800.

148. Food Stamps are claimed to have been used by a person in Michigan who won a $2 million lottery. Another Michigan resident reportedly purchased six lobsters, two porterhouse steaks, and five 24-packs of Mountain Dew using a Food Stamp debit card. Carleson Center for Public Policy, "Issue: Food Stamp Reform," retrieved November 30, 2011, http://theccpp.org/issues-food-stamp-reform.html.

149. Although a majority of Americans believe that a safety net should be provided for the poor, about two-thirds of Americans believe that

people become too dependent on the government. See Ron Haskins and Isabel Sawhill, *Creating An Opportunity Society*, Brookings Institution Press, Washington, DC, 2009 (especially Chapter 7, "Middle Class Complaints").

150. Ron Haskins, House Testimony, May 8, 2012, op cit.

151. Robert Greenstein, Center on Budgetary and Policy Priorities, testimony on "Strengthening the Safety Net," House Budget Committee, April 17, 2012.

152 National Conference of State Legislatures, "Children's Health Insurance Program (CHIP)," http://www.ncsl.org/issues-research/health/childrens-health-insurance-program-overview.aspx.

153. http://www.kff.org/medicaid/enrollmentreports.cfm.

154. The White House, *Creating Pathways to Opportunity*, October 2011, 9.

155. Amy Goldstein and N.C. Aizenmen, "House Votes to Repeal Health-Care Law," *Washington Post*, January 20, 2011; Jennifer Rubin, "Losing a Repeal Vote, But Winning the War Against Obama Care," *Washington Post*, February 3, 2011.

156. Center on Budget and Policy Priorities, http://www.cbpp.org/cms/index.cfm?fa=view&id=600.

157. Center on Budget and Policy Priorities, http://www.cbpp.org/cms/index.cfm?fa=view&id=936.

158. Even under AFDC, states rarely adjusted benefits to reflect inflation (see R. Kent Weaver, *Ending Welfare as We Know It*).

159. Center on Budget and Policy Priorities: http://www.cbpp.org/cms/index.cfm?fa=view&id=3534.

160. Danilo Treasi and LaDonna Pavetti, "TANF as a Weakening Safety Net for Poor Families," Center on Budget and Policy Priorities, 2012, http://www.cbpp.org/cms/index.cfm?fa=view&id=3700.

161. Pamela Loprest and Austin Nichols, "Dynamics of Being Disconnected," The Urban Institute, 2012, http://www.urban.org/uploadedpdf/412393-Dynamics-of-Being-Disconnected-from-Work-and-TANF.pdf.

162. Liz Schott, "Opportunities under the TANF Emergency Fund Created By the Federal Recovery Act," Center on Budget and Policy Priorities, 2009, http://www.cbpp.org/cms/index.cfm?fa=view&id=2878.

163. Liz Schott and LaDonna Pavetti, "Walking Away from a Win-Win-Win," Center for Budget and Policy Priorities, 2010, http://www.cbpp.org/cms/index.cfm?fa=view&id=3274.

164. Ron Haskins, House Testimony, May 8, 2012, op cit.

165. Introduction to Supplemental Security Income, http://www.cbpp.org/files/PolicyBasics_SocSec-IntroToSSI.pdf.

166. Jane Waldfogel, "The War on Poverty and the Safety Net for Families with Children," May 2012, http://npc.umich.edu/news/events/war-on-poverty-june-conference/waldfogel.pdf.

167. Lucie Schmidt, "Effects of Welfare Reform on the Supplemental Security Income (SSI) Program," *Policy Brief,* National Poverty Center, 2004.

168. Center on Budget and Policy Priorities, "Policy Basics: An Introduction to the Supplemental Security Income Program," 2011, http://www.cbpp.org/cms/index.cfm?fa=view&id=3370.

169. Social Security, Monthly Statistical Snapshot, May 2012, http://www.ssa.gov/policy/docs/quickfacts/stat_snapshot/, retrieved July 8, 2012.

170. Ron Haskins, "The SSI Program for Children: Time for Change? The Future of Children," *Policy Brief,* Princeton-Brookings, Spring 2012, http://futureofchildren.org/futureofchildren/publications/docs/22_01_PolicyBrief.pdf

171. Mark Duggan and Melissa S. Kearney, "The Impact of Child SSI Enrollment on Household Outcomes: Evidence from the Survey of Income and Program Participation," *Working Paper* 11568, August 2005, http://www.nber.org/papers/w11568.

172. Social Security Administration, *Facts and Figures about Social Security, 2011, Number of SSI Recipients, 1974–2010,* http://www.ssa.gov/policy/docs/chartbooks/fast_facts/2011/fast_facts11.html.

173. Richard Burkhauser, "Supplemental Security Income—Disabled Children: Time for Fundamental Change," testimony prepared for the House Ways and Means Subcommittee on Human Resources, 2011, http://www.aei.org/article/supplemental-security-income--disabled-children-time-for-fundamental-change/.

174. U.S. Government Accountability Office, "Older Adults and the 2007–2009 Recession," 2011, http://www.gao.gov/new.items/d1276.pdf

175. H. Stephen Kaye, "The Impact of the 2007–09 Recession on Workers with Disabilities," *Monthly Labor Review Online,* 2010, http://www.bls.gov/opub/mlr/2010/10/art2exc.htm

176. Ron Haskins, "The SSI Program for Children: Time for Change? The Future of Children," *Policy Brief,* Princeton-Brookings, Spring 2012.

177. Center on Budget and Policy Priorities, http://www.cbpp.org/files/4–13–11hous-US.pdf. The other federal programs that serve the remaining 600,000 households include: Housing for Elderly and People with Disabilities, RAP/Rent Supplement Program, Section 8 Moderate Rehabilitation, and USDA Section 521 Rental Assistance.

178. U.S. Department of Housing and Urban Development at http://portal.hud.gov/hudportal/HUD?src=/topics/rental_assistance/phprog

179. Ibid.

180. U.S. Department of Housing and Urban Development at http://portal.hud.gov/hudportal/HUD?src=/topics/housing_choice_voucher_program_section_8.

181. Authors' calculation from OMB Public Budget Database at http://www.gpoaccess.gov/usbudget/browse.html. See also the report on Section 8 rental assistance programs by the Center on Budget and Policy Priorities: http://www.cbpp.org/files/7–20–11hous.pdf.

182. http://www.cbpp.org/files/10–12–11hous.pdf.

183. HOPE VI is a plan by HUD to revitalize the worst public housing projects, by converting them into mixed-income developments. Studies have found that the number of newly built units in mixed-income areas is far less than the number of units torn down, thus causing a permanent reduction in the housing stock for low-income people. The Urban Institute, *A Decade of Hope IV: Research Findings and Policy Challenges*, May 2004, http://www.urban.org/uploadedpdf/411002_HOPEVI.pdf; also see http://www.cbpp.org/files/10–12–11hous.pdf.

184. Douglas McIntyre, "The 10 Best States for Unemployment Benefits—and the 10 Worst," *FOXbusiness.com*, May 12, 2011, http://www.foxbusiness.com/personal-finance/2011/05/12/10-best-states-unemployment-benefits-10-worst/.

185. U.S. Department of Labor, Bureau of Labor Statistics, Washington, DC, November 22, 2011, http://www.bls.gov/news.release/laws.nrO.htm. http://www.bls.gov/news.release/laus.nr0.htm/.

186. Figures presented in this paragraph come from authors' tabulations of data from the Bureau of Labor Statistics, http://www.doleta.gov/unemploy/chartbook.cfm. Also see Janet Hook and Kristina Peterson, "Congress Wrestles with 2012 Unemployment Benefits Extension," *Wall Street Journal*, November 30, 2011, http://blogs.wsj.com/economics/2011/11/30/congress-wrestles.

187. Center for Budget and Policy Priorities, http://www.cbpp.org/cms/index.cfm?fa=view&id=517.

188. The White House, *Creating Pathways to Opportunity*, October 2011, 6.

189. Bruce D. Meyer and James X. Sullivan, "The Material Well Being of the Poor and Middle Class Since 1980," *AEI Working Paper* #2011–04, October 25, 2011, 29.

190. Catherine Rampell, "Jobless Rate Dips to Lowest Level in More than Two Years," *New York Times*, 12/3/11.

191. Shaila Dewan, "U.S. Winds Down Longer Benefits for the Unemployed," *The New York Times*, 5/28/12.

192. On the case for extension, see Heidi Shierholz and Lawrence Mishel, "Labor Market Will Lose Over Half a Million Jobs If UI Extensions Expire in 2012," *Issue Brief* #318, Economic Policy Institute, November 4, 2011.

193. Shaila Dewan, Id.

194. Gary Burtless and Tracy Gordon, "The Federal Stimulus Programs and Their Effects," in *The Great Recession* (David B. Grusky, Bruce Western, Christopher Wimer, Eds.), Russell Sage Foundation, New York, 2011, 270.

195. Ibid., 269.

196. Internal Revenue Service, http://www.irs.gov/individuals/article/0,,id=150513,00.html. Also see the Tax Policy Center, http://www.taxpolicycenter.org/taxfacts/displayafact.cfm?DocID=36&Topic2id=40&Topic3id=42.

197. http://www.taxpolicycenter.org/taxtopics/conference_EITC.cfm .

Chapter 5

198. Coalition on Human Needs, "Self-Inflicted Wounds: Protecting Families and Our Economy from Bad Budget Choices," *Report by the Coalition on Human Needs*, updated April 2012.

199. Robert E. Hall, "Fiscal Stimulus," *Daedalus*, Fall 2010, 93; also see The Committee for a Responsible Federal Budget, February 17, 2011, http://crfb.org/blogs/happy-second-birthday-arra (review of professional estimates of the impact of the Recovery Act on GDP and employment). Also see Alan S. Blinder and Mark Zandi, *How The Great Recession Was Brought to an End*, July 27, 2010.

200. Ibid.

201. For the Obama administration's view of how the 2009 stimulus package and other recent initiatives have helped the poor, see The White House, *Creating Pathways to Opportunity*, October 2011.

202. For an account suggesting that the Recovery Act prevented a larger rise in poverty in 2009, see Arloc Sherman, "Poverty and Financial Distress Would Have Been Substantially Worse in 2010 Without Government Action, New Census Data Show," Center for Budget and Policy Priorities, 2011, http://www.cbpp.org/cms/index.cfm?fa=view&id=3610.

203. Jesse Bricker, Brian Bucks, Arthur Kennickell, Traci Mach, and Kevin Moore, "Surveying the Aftermath of the Storm: Changes in Family Finances from 2007 to 2009," *Finance and Economics Discussion Series* 2011–17, Board of Governors of Federal Reserve System, March 2011, http://www.federalreservesystem.gov/pubs/feds/2011/201117/index.html.

204. Jesse Bricker, Arthur B. Kennickell, Kevin B. Moore, and John Sabelhaus. "Changes in Family Finances from 2007 to 2010: Evidence from the Survey of Consumer Finances," *Federal Reserve Bulletin*, 98(2), June 2012, http://www.federalreserve.gov/pubs/bulletin/2012/PDF/scf12.pdf.

205. OMB, Budget of the U.S. Government, Fiscal Year 2012, Historical Tables, 1.1.

206. Damian Paletta, "White House Expects Deficit to Spike to $1.65 Trillion," *Wall Street Journal*, February 14, 2011.

207. U.S. Congressional Budget Office, letter from CBO Director Douglas W. Elmendorf to Honorable John Boehner and Honorable Harry Reid, August 1, 2011 (hereafter cited as "CBO Letter, August 1, 2011."

208. National Women's Law Center, http://www.nwlc.org/resource/unbalanced-debt-ceiling-deal-cuts-vital-programs-critical-fights-ahead, August 1, 2011.

209. http://rules.house.gov/Media/file/PDF_112_1/Floor_Text/DEBT_016_xml.pdf.

210. National Women's Law Center, Id.

211. http://www.dailykos.com/story/2011/08/08/1004494/-Five-Things-You-Need-to-Know.

212. CBO Letter, August 1, 2011, 6.

213. CBO Letter, August 1, 2011, 7.

214. National Women's Law Center, Id.

215. Donna Cassata, "Defense Hawks Insist on Halting Military Cuts," *USA Today*, November 22, 2011.

216. Julie Vogtman, National Women's Law Center, "Five Things You Need to Know About the Debt Ceiling Deal," August 8, 2011.

217. Melanie Grayce West, "A Hunger for Funding," *Wall Street Journal*, November 28, 2011, R6.

218. Tamar Lewin, "Budget Cuts Threaten Access to College Placement Tests,"*New York Times*, March 12, 2012, A11.

219. College Financial Aid Advisors, Pell Grant Cuts for 2012–13, May 21, 2012, http://collegefinancialaidadvisors.com.

220. Ann Carrns. Student Loans Face Rate Rise. *New York Times*. March 17, 2012, B4.

221. Claudio Sanchez. Student Loan Deal Pales Against Other Education Cuts. June 30, 2012, http://www.npr.org/2012/06/30/156024236/the-flip-slide. . . retrieved 7/3/2012.

222. Damian Paletta and Janet Hook, "Senate Passes Farm Bill that Curtails Aid," June 21, 2012, http://online.wsj.com/article/SB1000142405 27023048987045774808027262668554.html; Food Research and Action Center, "Farm Bill Preserves Strong SNAP Structure; Makes Unnecessary and Harmful Cuts to Benefits," June 21, 2012, http://org2.

democracyinaction.org/o/5118/p/salsa/web/common/public/
content?content_ite. . . retrieved July 9, 2012.

223. CBO Letter, August 1, 2011, 1, 3–4.

224. Paul Davidson, "Regulators Combat Unemployment Insurance Waste and Fraud," *USA Today*, July 5, 2011, http://abcnews.go.com/Business/regulators-combat-unemployment-insurance-waste-fraud. . .

225. U.S. General Accountability Office, "Medicare and Medicaid Fraud, Waste and Abuse: Effective Implementation of Recent Laws and Agency Actions Could Help Reduce Improper Payments," GAO-11–409T, March 9, 2011, http:www.gao.gov/products/GAO-11–409T.

226. Kathryn Nix, "Waste, Fraud, and Abuse in Medicare and Medicaid Still Await Solutions," Heritage Foundation, March 10, 2011, http://blog.heritage.org/2011/03/10/waste-fraud-and-abuse-in-medicare-and medicaid-still. . .

227. The White House, "We Can't Wait: Agencies Cut Nearly $18 Billion in Improper Payments, Announce New Steps for Stopping Government Waste," November 15, 2011.

228. Marisol Bello, "States Restrict Welfare Buying," *USA Today*, July 9, 2012, http://www.usatoday.com/news/nation/story/2012–07–08/welfare-purchase-restrictions/56100508/1.

229. Kaiser Commission on Medicaid and the Uninsured, "Update: State Budgets in Recession and Recovery," *Policy Brief*, October 2011, 1.

230. Nicole Bullock and James Politi, "US States Warned to Tackle Fiscal Threats," *Financial Times*, July 18, 2012, 8.

231. Gary Burtless and Tracy Gordon, "The Federal Stimulus Programs and Their Effects," in *The Great Recession* (David B. Grusky, Bruce Western, and Christopher Wimer, Eds.), Russell Sage Foundation, New York, 2011, 280.

232. Elizabeth McNichol, Phil Oliff, and Nicholas Johnson, "States Continue to Feel Recession's Impact," Center on Budget and Policy Priorities, updated March 21, 2012. http://www.cbpp.org/cms/?fa=view&id=711.

233. Tami Luhby, "State, Local Layoffs Hit Record Levels," CNN.com, June 6, 2011; Tamy Luhby, "Government Workers Catch Break," CNN.com, August 5, 2011, http://money.cnn.com/2011/08/05/news/economy/government_jobs/index.htm.

234. N. C. Aizenman, "State Spending on Medicaid Up Sharply," *Washington Post*, October 27, 2011.

235. Peter Suderman, "States Still Struggling to Pay for Medicaid," http://reason.com/blog/2011/11/28/states-still-struggling-to-pay-for-medic.

236. Kaiser Commission on Medicaid and the Uninsured, "Impact of the Medicaid Fiscal Relief Provisions in the American Recovery and Reinvestment Act (ARRA)," *Policy Brief,* October 2011, 6–8.

237. Jason Dean and Howard Packowitz, "Governor of Illinois Urges Cuts to Medicaid" *Wall Street Journal,* February 23, 2012, A6.

238. Associated Press, "Generous No More, Illinois Cuts Medicaid Spending," June 14, 2012, http://dailyherald.com/article/20120614/news/7061498831 (no longer available).

239. Casandra Andrews, "Children's Programs Spared from New Alabama Medicaid Cuts," May 18, 2012, http://blog.al.com/live/2012/05/childrens_programs_spared_from.html.

240. Associated Press, "California's Budget Deal Cuts Welfare, Health Care," June 21, 2012, http://www.foxnews.com/us/2012/06/21/california-budget-deal-cuts-welfare-health-care/ retrieved July 9, 2012.

241. http://www.cbpp.org/cms/index.cfm?fa=view&id=3534.

242. Christina Jewett, "State Revisits Budget as Prior Cuts Hit Poor, Disabled," *California Watch,* May 18, 2011, http://californiawatch.org/dailyreport/state-revisits-budget-prior-cuts-hit-poor-disabled-10328.

243. Associated Press, op cit.

244. Jason DeParle, "Welfare Limits Left Poor Adrift as Recession Hit," *New York Times,* April 7, 2012. http://www.nytimes.com/2012/04/08/us/welfare-limits-left-poor-adrift-as-recession-hit.html?pagewanted=all.

245. Ibid.

246. Monica Davey, "Families Feel Sharp Edge of State Budget Cuts," *New York Times,* September 6, 2011.

247. Center on Budget and Policy Priorities, http:www.cbpp.org/cms/index.cfm?fa=view&id=3550.

Chapter 6

248. Ben Polak and Peter Schott, "America's Hidden Austerity Program," *New York Times Economix Blog,* June 11, 2012, http://economix.blogs.nytimes.com/2012/06/11/americas-hidden-austerity-program/.

249. Richard Wolf, "Fewer Draw on Federal Support," *USA Today,* May 29, 2012, A1.

250. U.S. Congressional Budget Office, "The Supplemental Nutrition Assistance Program," April 2012, 1.

251. Charles O. Jones, *The Presidency in a Separated System,* Second Edition, Brookings, Washington, DC, 2005.

252. Ron Haskins, "Combating Poverty: Understanding New Challenges for Families," testimony to U.S. Senate Committee on Finance,

June 5, 2012, http://www.brookings.edu/research/
testimony/2012/06/05-poverty-families-haskins/

253. Stuart Butler, Alison Acosta Fraser, and William Beach, "Saving the American Dream: The Heritage Plan to Fix the Debt, Cut Spending, and Restore Prosperity," *Special Report* #91, The Heritage Foundation, May 10, 2011.

254. Bender et al., Ibid., 16 (current means testing in Social Security); 20 (current means testing in Medicare).

255. Stuart Butler, Alison Acosta Fraser, and William Beach, Id.

256. Dean Baker and Hye Jin Rho, "The Potential Savings to Social Security from Means Testing," Center for Economic and Policy Research, Washington, DC, March 2011, 13.

257. Robert Rubin, "A Budget Grand Bargain Will Follow the Election," *Wall Street Journal*, May 29, 2012, A13.

258. U.S. Congressional Budget Office, "CBO's 2011 Long-Term Budget Outlook," June 22, 2011, Corrected, February 29, 2012.

259. Without reform of entitlement programs (such as Social Security, Medicare, Medicaid, SNAP), there is not enough spending left in the federal budget to resolve the fiscal crisis. Stuart Butler et al., "Saving the American Dream," May 10, 2011, 8 (Chart 3).

260. Pam Fessler, "'Social Safety Net' Less Safe as Cuts Debated," March 5, 2011. http://www.npr.org/2011/03/05/134265932/social-safety-net-less-safe -as-congress-debates...

261. Ron Haskins, House testimony, May 8, 2012; Senate testimony, June 5, 2012, op cit.

262. D. Andrew Austin and Mindy R. Levit, "Mandatory Spending Since 1962," *CRS Report to Congress* 7–5700. March 23, 2012, RL22074, Table 2, 7.

263. Martha R. Burt and Demetra Smith Nightingale, "Repairing the U.S. Social Safety Net," Urban Institute Press, Washington, DC, 2010, 57.

264. Bureau of Labor Statistics, "Characteristics of Minimum Wage Workers: 2010." http://www.bls.gov/cps/minwage2010.htm.

265. http://www.usinflationcalculator.com/inflation/historical-inflation-rates/.

266. David Card and Alan B. Kruegar, "Minimum Wages and Employment: A Case Study of the Fast Food Industry in New Jersey and Pennsylvania: A Reply," *American Economic Review* 84(4), September 1994,772–793; "A Reply," *American Economic Review* 90(5), December 2000, 1397–1420; also see Sylvia A. Allegretto, Arindrajit Dube, and Michael Reich, "Do Minimum Wages Really Reduce Teen Employment? Accounting for Heterogeneity and Selectivity in Panel Data. Industrial Relations," 50(2), April 2011, 205–240.

267. The Post's View, "Romney's Timely Proposal to Raise and Index the Minimum Wage," *Washington Post*, February 2, 2012, http://www.washingtonpost.com/opinions/a-timely-proposal-to-raise-and-index-the-minimum.

268. Robert D. Plotnick, "The Alleviation of Poverty: How Far Have We Come?," in *Oxford Handbook of the Economics of Poverty* (Philip N. Jefferson, Ed.), January 2011 (draft), in press.

269. Anna Wilde Mathews, "Medicaid Cuts Rile Doctors," *Wall Street Journal*, February 24, 2012, A3.

270. Kaiser Commission on Medicaid and the Uninsured, "Medicaid and Managed Care: Key Data, Trends and Issues," *Policy Brief*, February 2010.

271. Kaiser Commission on Medicaid and the Uninsured, "Medicaid Managed Care: Key Data, Trends and Issues," *Policy Brief*, February 2012

272. Phil Galewitz, "Medicaid Managed Care Programs Grow; So Do Issues," *USA Today*. November 12, 2010.

273. U.S. Congressional Budget Office, "Trends in the Distribution of Household Income Between 1979 and 2007," Washington, DC, October 2011, 21.

274. John Merline, "The Richest 1% Get $10 Billion a Year from Uncle Sam," *Investor's Business Daily*, December 13, 2011.

275. Dean Baker and Hye Jin Rho, "The Potential Savings to Social Security from Means Testing," Center for Economic Research, Washington, DC, March 2011, 1, 4 (Table 1).

276. U.S. Congressional Budget Office, "Trends in the Distribution of Household Income Between 1997 and 2007," Washington, DC, October 2011, Appendix C, Table C-1, 45.

277. For a wealthy columnist's case against further means testing of Social Security, see Allan Sloan, "'Means Testing' to Bolster Social Security? It's Already Happening," March 1, 2012, http://www.washingtonpost.com/business/economy/means-testing-to-bolster-social-security...

278. Andrew G. Biggs, "Means Testing and Its Limits," *National Affairs*, http://www.nationalaffairs.com/publications/detail/means-testing-and-its-limits, accessed May 22, 2012.

279. Ibid.

280. For the case that Medicaid eligibility is not generous enough, see Robert Greenstein, Center on Budget and Policy Priorities, testimony on "Strengthening the Safety Net," hearing before the House Budget Committee, April 17, 2012, 11.

281. U.S. Congressional Budget Office, The Supplemental Nutrition Assistance Program, April 2012, 2.

282. U.S. Congressional Budget Office, Ibid, 8–9.

283. John Merline, "The Richest 1% Get $10 Billion a Year from Uncle Sam," *Investor's Business Daily*, December 13, 2011.

284. Ken Bensinger, "Owning a Car is Key to Getting Off Public Assistance, Study Finds," *Los Angeles Times*, March 14, 2012, B2.

285. Danilo Trisi and LaDonna Pavetti, "TANF Weakening as a Safety Net for Poor Families," 2012, http://www.cbpp.org/cms/index.cfm?fa=view&id=3700.

286. For more information on participation requirements, see Heather Hahn, David Kassabian, and Sheila Zedlewski, "TANF Work Requirements and State Strategies to Meet Them," 2012, The Urban Institute, http://www.acf.hhs.gov/programs/opre/other_resrch/tanf_ccdf/reports/work_requirements.pdf.

287. Ibid.

288. Danilo Trisi and LaDonna Pavetti,op cit.

289. U.S. Department of Labor, "Comparison of State Unemployment Laws," undated, http://workforcesecurity.doleta.gov/unemploy/uilaw-compar/2009/comparison2009.asp.

290. Chad Stone, Robert Greenstein, and Martha Coven, "Addressing Long Standing Gaps in Unemployment Insurance Coverage," 2007, http://www.cbpp.org/cms/index.cfm?fa=view&id=517.

291. Ibid.

292. U.S. Government Accountability Office, "Unemployment Insurance: Economic Circumstances of Individuals Who Exhausted Benefits," 2012, http://www.gao.gov/assets/590/588680.pdf.

293. Office of the Press Secretary, White House, "White House Announces Details on President's Plan to Provide Americans with Job Training and Employment Services, "March 12, 2012, http://www.whitehouse.gov/the-press-office/2012/03/12/white-house-announces-details-president-s-plan-provide-americans-job-tra...

294. David Muhlhausen, "Put the Ineffective Department of Labor Job Training Programs on the Chopping Block," February 15, 2011, http://blog.heritage.org/2011/02/15/put-the-ineffective-department-of-labor-job-training-programs-on-the-chopping-block/.

295. Harry Holzer, "Raising Job Quality and Skills for American Workers: Creating More-Effective Education and Workforce Development Systems in the States," Brookings Institution, 2011.

296. Ibid.

297. Testimony of Robert Greenstein, President, Center on Budget and Policy Priorities, "Strengthening the Safety Net," House Budget Committee, United States Congress. April 17, 2012.

298. U.S. Congressional Budget Office, "The Supplemental Nutrition Assistance Program," April 2012, 3–4 (including Figure 2).

299. Alan S. Blinder, "The Long and Short of Fiscal Policy," *Wall Street Journal*, May 22, 2012, A17.

300. Testimony of Robert Greenstein, President, Center on Budget and Policy Priorities, "Strengthening the Safety Net," House Budget Committee, United States Congress, April 17, 2012, 5–6.

301. Robert Greenstein and Richard Kogan, "A Constitutional Balanced Budget Amendment Threatens Great Economic Damage," 2011, http://www.cbpp.org/cms/index.cfm?fa=view&id=3509.

Index

KRISTIN S. SEEFELDT is Assistant Professor of Social Work at the University of Michigan and author of *Working after Welfare: How Women Balance Jobs and Family in the Wake of Welfare Reform* and *Welfare Reform*.

JOHN D. GRAHAM is Dean of the Indiana University School of Public and Environmental Affairs and author of *Bush on the Home Front: Domestic Policy Triumphs and Setbacks* (IUP, 2010). From 2001 to 2006 he served as Administrator of the Office of Information and Regulatory Affairs, White House Office of Management and Budget.

CPSIA information can be obtained at www.ICGtesting.com
Printed in the USA
LVOW042351030113

314302LV00001B/1/P